Second-string Heroes,
First-class Saints

Second-string Heroes, First-class Saints

Character Studies in the
Book of Acts

by
Harold Bonner

Beacon Hill Press of Kansas City
Kansas City, Missouri

ISBN: 083-411-3333

Printed in the
United States of America

Cover Design: Crandall Vail

Permission to quote from the following copyrighted versions is acknowledged with
appreciation:

The Holy Bible, New International Version (NIV), copyright © 1973, 1978, 1984 by
the International Bible Society.

The Living Bible (TLB), © 1971 by Tyndale House Publishers, Wheaton, Ill.

10   9   8   7   6   5   4   3   2   1

Contents

Preface

God speaks to us through the lives of His people. As we observe His grace at work in them, we begin to understand better how His grace would work in us. It is the most beautiful story ever told—what God does in the lives of those who give Him a chance.

That beauty is readily seen in the lives of those early Christians whom we meet in the pages of the Book of Acts. Few of them were granted any measure of fame, but each of them became an example of holy living, a portrait of what God can do with ordinary people who would love Him supremely and serve Him faithfully.

The 13 character studies that are presented in these pages convey that message. While they were one in their common commitment to Jesus Christ, they individually reflect the wide range of gifts and graces that make up the Body of Christ. The natural emphasis out of each life is different, and that variety adds more beauty to the miracle of God's redeeming work in Jesus.

The format has been chosen intentionally so that where it might be so desired, this book might serve for a quarter of study or discussion. Obviously, there are other individuals in the Book of Acts who were not selected. Those chosen are inspiring examples who were not in the select group of Christ's first disciples, but who, by His grace and their faithfulness, became what we might call indeed "first-class saints."

1

Matthias:
Shining in the Shadows

Acts 1:15–26

Not everybody is a star, even though most everybody would like to be in some worthy way. Some are, and they set the records by which the rest of us are measured. Bo Jackson, Heisman trophy winner from Auburn University, shocked the football world by turning down his professional football contract to sign a baseball contract with the Kansas City Royals. Bo is good. When he first signed, he drew crowds to Kansas City's stadium, just to see him take batting practice. He probably hit more balls out of the park that day than our team at Pasadena College was allotted for an entire season of play. And then Bo decided to add professional football after all, playing with the Los Angeles Raiders when the Royals finish their schedule. Some guys have it all.

Some are stars . . . that way from the beginning. But most of us are ordinary. In the language of professional sports we are never "drafted." If we make the team, it is because we show up and stay at it and don't give up. Most of us know the feeling the late Bob Benson wrote about . . . about being the last chosen . . . and sent out to "deep right field."

When Jesus Christ walked the earth, He chose 12 men to be with Him. He called them disciples. We call them that too;

7

we also call them apostles. They were His "first string." They were His "first round draft picks." The Gospels center around Him and them. And of the 12 there was the most valuable circle of Peter, James, and John . . . and there was the infamous failure of Judas.

But in the Book of Acts there come into the roster of the redeemed some new names in the lineup, men and women who stand alongside of Peter, James, and John. And while perhaps they may be in the shadow of the 12, yet in their own way and time they have, by the grace of God, emerged as first-class saints. They are our kind of people, those second-string heroes; those first-class saints. They tell us there is room on His team for everyone who really determines to walk with Him.

So think about Matthias: shining in the shadows.

I. NOTE THE SETTING

It was an uncertain, fragile, exciting time for that company of first believers that we read about in Acts 1. Here we read of the ascension of Jesus. His atoning death and resurrection were fresh history, only 40 days old. It had been a month and a half filled with incredible lows of failure and despair, incredible highs of intermittent fellowship with the assuring Savior, and haunting loneliness in between. Jesus, having established for them beyond doubt the reality of His resurrection and with that the unshakable conviction of His deity, then ascended in glory. He was gone, leaving them with a promise of another Comforter, the Holy Spirit, and leaving them with the assignment to share the good news with the whole world (Acts 1:8).

Their number was just 120. Some estimate the world population of that time at 120 million. If so, that means the odds were "a million to one." In 1986 our world's people count went over the 5 billion figure, and that means our mission is just as much in need of divine power and grace as theirs.

But they did not give up, though the assignment was overwhelming. They did what Jesus told them to do . . . they went to prayer. T. B. Matson wrote, "The Christians who have turned the world upside down have been praying men and women with a vision in their hearts and the Bible in their hands." They were not sure; they did not know; but they were willing to take it one step at at time. That is all God asks. That is the meaning of discipleship . . . a "long obedience in the same direction."

II. NOTE THE PEOPLE
(Acts 1:15-26)

The last half of Acts 1 focuses on three names, the last one being the one we shall dwell on.

A. Peter. The first named is Peter (vv. 13, 15). Peter is named because he was the *forgiven one.* Six weeks earlier Peter was a classic failure. He had denied his Lord. He folded under the simple question of a quiet servant girl who had identified Peter as a follower of Jesus.

Peter cursed and lied. He denied that He even knew Jesus. And then he went out to cry. He with the loud mouth and the bragging style was after all a hollow man, a sham and a hypocrite.

But now, six weeks later, Peter is the leader. He is first named as one among the people at prayer (v. 13). He called the gathering to order, chaired the meeting, and set the agenda. Why? Peter was a forgiven man. It is a glorious thing to be forgiven, to have brought all of life to the feet of Jesus, and with a broken spirit and a repentant mind to ask Jesus to cover it with His blood and cleanse the mind-set that had brought it to pass. Forgiveness is not taking one's sins lightly; it is taking God's grace seriously. And forgiveness is what God offers freely in Jesus Christ (1 John 1:9). Wrote Charles Wesley:

9

> *Times without number have I pray'd,*
>   *"This only once forgive";*
> *Relapsing, when Thy hand was stay'd,*
>   *And suffer'd me to live:—*
>
> *Yet now the kingdom of Thy peace,*
>   *Lord, to my heart restore;*
> *Forgive my vain repentances*
>   *And bid me sin no more.* [1]

B. Judas. The second named is Judas (v. 16). He is mentioned because he is the *fallen one.* He betrayed the Lord Jesus into the hands of His executioners. He sold his Lord for 30 pieces of silver, the price of a slave. You would not sell your dog for that, but Judas, one of the dozen men that Jesus had singled out to be His closest companions, he did that. In remorse he took his own life, a suicide. But that is not the end. Verse 25 reminds us that "he went to his own place," not just the "field of blood" purchased by the conspiring leaders, but his own place of eternal hell and everlasting separation from God. Judas said in his life, "Not Thy will but mine be done." He got what he chose. People always do. Hell is just that.

C. Matthias. The third named is Matthias (vv. 23-26). He is named because he is the *filling one.* Peter saw in Psalm 69 and Psalm 109 biblical direction to have someone fill the empty place among the 12 disciples. They nominated two—Barsabbas and Matthias. They elected one. They chose Matthias, a second-string disciple, but a disciple nevertheless.

III. NOTE THE MAN

Some scorn Matthias. They say of him that he was never mentioned again after his election. That is true. The Bible gives us just this single moment of him. But don't write him off just because of that. Neither are 8 of the other 11 disciples ever mentioned again in scripture after this moment.

Some say that Peter was really out of order in calling for an election at that time, that God had someone else in mind. E. Stanley Jones believed the apostle Paul was the chosen one, that "greatest Christian" of the Early Church.

But I believe that Matthias, though indeed a "second-string hero" was every bit a first-class saint of God. I say that because of the modest but moving tribute to his life. The qualifications Peter had set for that special election for the replacement apostle were two: (1) a part of the larger group of believing ones from the beginning of the ministry of Jesus; and (2) a witness of the Resurrection (vv. 21-22).

That speaks to me about the faithfulness of Matthias. He had been there all the time. From those first days when Jesus began to proclaim the kingdom of God, Matthias had found his heart strangely attached to Jesus. He was never singled out for any special attention, but he never cut out, or dropped out. When the cause was popular, he was there. When the cause was unpopular and risky, he was there. When they nailed Jesus to the Cross, he was there, somewhere. When Jesus broke the bonds of death in Resurrection power, he was there. When Jesus ascended in glory, he was there.

Matthias was not privileged to the special place given to the first 12 that Jesus gathered around Him. But Matthias had a heart for Jesus, and the people knew it. He was faithful, not for ego but for love, not for honor but for service. He never gave up, and he never quit. Jesus was where his heart was, and, as the song says, "I guess it all comes down to where your heart is." For three long years he was there in that wider circle, doing what he could, being what he was. And when that company of 120 believers looked for someone whom they considered fit (or qualified) to become a disciple of Jesus, they chose Matthias.

We say it often, but we may not say it enough. However men count greatness, God counts greatness beginning with faithfulness. "It is required in stewards, that a man be found faithful" (1 Cor. 4:2). It is not ability that God prizes so much as it is availability. Matthias qualified. He was there, in the shadows, but in the shadows he was shining with the warm love of stedfastness.

Given the human disposition to fashion its heroes and to glorify its superstars—even in the kingdom of God—there is the temptation to dismiss the ordinary shoeleather grace of holy consistency. But God doesn't. He keeps saying, "Be thou faithful unto death, and I will give thee a crown of life" (Rev. 2:10). When the great Christian, who some think should have had the place granted Matthias (i.e., the apostle Paul), came down to the end of his earthly life, though his gifts were many and his record of service unequaled in the hall of faith, it was not that record that brought peace to his heart, but rather the grace of God that enabled him to be faithful.

Said the apostle Paul, "I am now ready to be offered, and the time of my departure is at hand. I have fought a good fight, I have finished my course, I have kept the faith: Henceforth there is laid up for me a crown of righteousness, which the Lord, the righteous judge shall give me at that day: and not to me only, but unto all them also that love his appearing" (2 Tim. 4:6-8).

Matthias was faithful, there from the beginning.

The other qualification of Matthias was that he was a witness to the resurrection of Jesus (v. 22). He was there all the time and ready to proclaim the heart of the gospel, that Jesus Christ is a living Savior. Matthias witnessed what only a few did—he saw Jesus in His risen glory; and Matthias testified to what all Christians must declare—I know Him in His living power.

It strikes me that for all of his commonness and lack of

superstar status, Matthias was what every Christian must be—
a faithful follower and a trustworthy witness. For after all, it is
not what we are but who Jesus is and who He is to us that is
the great treasure of the redeemed and the hope of the world
to which He sends us in rescue.

2

Barnabas:
The Courage to Encourage

Acts 4:33-37; 9:26-28; 11:19-30; 12:25—13:3;
15:38-40

A church official was going with his host pastor to a speaking engagement. As he drove, the host pastor gave directions, saying, "Turn right at the next intersection," but motioning left as he did so. The church leader made no comment but turned left and arrived at the destination. Later he remarked, "When there is a difference between what a man says and what he does, give attention to what he does. That is what he really means."

When people have to choose between what we say and what we do, they will choose the latter in a moment. They prefer "lived sermons" over "spoken sermons" any day.

It is early in our study of God's second-string heroes, first-class saints that we meet a man who must have possessed an extraordinary gift of eloquence, wisdom, and strength. After all, when the believers of the Christian community got to know him, they gave him a nickname. Kenneth Taylor in his *Living Bible* translates it as "Barny, the Preacher!" (Acts 4:36). But the truth is that there is no record of any sermon he preached, not even a word of one. His greater strength was the life he lived; his greater gift was the gift of encouragement.

14

That is the repeated role he fills in the Scripture. So let's think about that. If Matthias speaks about faithfulness, then Barnabas speaks about the courage to encourage. We certainly can use all of the people like Barnabas we can find.

I. CONSIDER THE RECORD OF BARNABAS

By any standard of measure, Barnabas was one of the truly great men of the Bible. We know nothing of his life before he came to faith in Jesus Christ save the facts mentioned in his first introduction in Scripture (Acts 4:36-37). But then that should not bother us, for a man's greatness is not his "B.C." but his "A.D."

We are told his real name was Joses, or Joseph, and that his home was on the island of Cyprus. He is also identified as one of the tribe of Levi, which means that he grew up with a definite sense of responsibility in the ongoing of Jewish worship where he lived. He was a leader among his brethren. And more than that, Joseph whom we know as Barnabas was wealthy. How wealthy we do not know, but he had land. Not bad for a man of a tribe who in the time of Canaan distribution received no land but instead had the Lord for their inheritance.

How he came to faith in Christ, when he came, or who shared personal faith with him we are not told. But the results ring with the genuineness of redemption.

For one thing, he sold land and gave money from the sale into the Christian treasury (Acts 4:37). The exemplary stewardship of Barnabas stands in blessed contrast with the scheming deceit of Ananias and Sapphira whose shame is told in the next verses. Obviously, the mere giving of money does not of itself make one a Christian, nor can it ever purchase salvation. But when a man goes with God, his pocketbook must go along also. And since God really had Barnabas, he had his wallet also.

Other good things happened too. They are hinted at in the

new name the Christian brothers gave him—no longer Joseph, but Barnabas, the son of consolation, the son of comfort, the son of exhortation—all of which suggest that he was a man who proclaimed the Christian message with grace, wisdom, and power.

In Acts 11:24 we are told he was "a good man, . . . full of the Holy Ghost and of faith." That figures, for the Holy Spirit is never far from a man who is trying to be what God wants him to be. The Holy Spirit is the Author of all spiritual success. Without Him, we could not even confess Jesus Christ as our Savior (1 Cor. 12:3), but in Him there is a fullness of salvation in entire sanctification (2 Thess. 2:13). Those Christians gave a new name for an old one, because God by the Holy Spirit had made a new man out of an old one.

When Paul was converted, he became literally "a man without a country": hated by his own countrymen, who counted him a traitor; suspected by the Christian community, who feared him to be a spy and shunned him like a plague. But one stepped forward to befriend the former terrorizer of the church. It was Barnabas. He took his stand with Paul and let Paul benefit from his own reputation until Paul had built a reputation of his own.

Years passed. When the Christian community in Antioch experiencd the outbreak of revival with large numbers of Gentile converts, the church at Jerusalem sent Barnabas to assess the developments and stabilize the work. It was Barnabas who discerned both the opportunity and role one man might fill in it as no other. That man was Paul—unheard of now for some seven years. Barnabas went to Tarsus and brought Paul to Antioch where Paul's public ministry began. What perception; what power! Little wonder that the name "Christian" was first used in Antioch (Acts 11:26) where Barnabas helped the greatest preacher-missionary-theologian the Church has ever known fill the place for which God had prepared him.

So fervent was the zeal of the Antioch church that the vision of reaching a lost world came alive there rather than at Jerusalem. The voice of the Spirit was to "separate . . . Barnabas and Saul for the work whereunto I have called them" (Acts 13:2). At first it was Barnabas—and Saul. What a tribute to the Levite from Cyprus. And then, in time, it became Paul and Barnabas (v. 13), but there is no record that Barnabas even noticed the emergence of Paul above him. Evidently he cared little about who received the credit, so long as the work of God went forward.

The last reference to him in the Book of Acts (15:36-40) records the determination of Barnabas to help young Mark regain the place in the mission of the church that he had forfeited by abandoning Paul and Barnabas in the midst of the first missionary journey (13:13). Barnabas would believe in Mark just as he had believed in Paul. And that belief, in both cases, would help provide the work of Christ with two of its finest leaders.

II. Consider the Lesson from Barnabas

The only words in Scripture directly assigned to Barnabas are words jointly assigned to him and Paul—words in which they deny that they possess any deity and in which they simply declare their common humanity (Acts 14:15). But what a special man he was. His life was the most powerful of preachers. In stewardship, in leadership, in wisdom, Barnabas reflected the stedfastness of disciplined dignity. No wonder they called him the "son of exhortation."

The thing that stands out more than any other, however, in the life of Barnabas—more than the land he gave to the Church or the missionary travels he took, more than anything —was his personal ministry of encouragement to those who needed it.

If the Church owes Paul to the example of Stephen, it also owes Paul to the encouragement of Barnabas. Not just in that beginning hour when no one believed his testimony (Acts 9) but in that later hour (some 10 years after his conversion) when no one was using his gifts—in both crucial times—it was Barnabas who had the courage to encourage. He said by life as well as by words, "I believe you, Paul, and I believe in you. Let me walk with you as Jesus uses you."

Without Barnabas and his personal encouragement, Paul could well have been lost to the Church. How impoverished the faith would be without all that Paul did and all that Paul wrote. Without Barnabas and his personal encouragement, Mark could well have been lost to the Church. How impoverished the faith would be without his Gospel record of the life of Christ, and his participation in the Early Church leadership.

Surely Barnabas belongs on the roster of God's second-string heroes who were truly first-class saints. He gave the Church his wealth, he gave Paul his friendship, he gave Antioch his presence, he gave the Gentile world his energy, he gave Mark his companionship, he gave the Lord his life—and he gave to all of us the lesson of the beauty of encouragment, worked out in the exhausting but exciting challenges of life.

III. FOLLOW THE EXAMPLE OF BARNABAS

What a need there is for a continuing company of souls who like Barnabas touch the world that touches them with the renewal of confidence and courage. Goodness knows how the daily grind takes its toll on man's spirit. It can be economic setback, domestic conflict, poor health, professional disappointment, shattered relationships, or a host of other monsters. When life is difficult confidence and courage are hard-pressed. Who hasn't at some time, felt like the Psalmist when he cried, "I looked on my right hand, and beheld, but there was no man that would know me: refuge failed me; no man cared for my soul" (Ps. 142:4).

Little wonder then that God in His wisdom has called His people to the ministry of encouragement (see Rom. 12:8, NIV), a Christian life-style of awareness and uplift that touches others with renewed "heart." How often have our own lives been touched by the lift of another's life and love. The greater question for us is, "Is my life a source of encouragement right now to someone else? If so, who? If so, how?"

Randal Denny has seen an illustration of this in the beautiful redwoods of northern California. He writes: "The great Pacific Coast redwood trees are the tallest trees in the world. Some of them are 300 feet high and more than 2,500 years old. Most other trees have a root system which goes as deep as the tree is tall. But not the redwoods! Their root systems are dependent upon the surface water of rainfall. Since their roots are so shallow, one finds them growing only in groves. The roots of all the trees in the grove intertwine, locking themselves together. Redwoods can withstand the storms because they are not standing alone. They support and protect each other."[1]

It takes courage to encourage; it takes "heart" to give "heart." But then isn't that what life in Christ is about? Barnabas would teach us that it is.

3

Stephen:
Reflecting Christ Our Lord

Acts 6:5–15

It is a common temptation in the human family to envy others for their successes—possessions, positions, and pleasures. But it is no temptation at all to envy anyone the disciplines, sacrifices, or industry that may have been necessary to achieve those successes.

Since Mother Teresa of Calcutta has been spotlighted and publicized for her nearly 60 years of selfless service to the poor of Calcutta, even honored with the Nobel Peace prize for her life of charity, she has generated in the minds of multitudes similar ideas. Because of her many ask themselves, "Could I be like that, a humble heroine of the world?"

Personally, I doubt there are many who yearn for the sacrifice that has brought Mother Teresa to this hour. We are impressed with her work—feeding 50,000 starving people a day. We are impressed that her work has attracted 2,500 other nuns and priests. We are impressed that she has achieved superstar status, with access to kings and presidents, but the price—that is something else.

Mother Teresa's life since she went to Calcutta at the age of 18 with little help and a great vision has been rugged. She rises each morning at 4 A.M. and works tirelessly throughout the day before retiring at 1 A.M. for three hours of sleep. Then another day of living to give begins. That price seems so high, and the human spirit quickly looks for an easier way.

There is something of that in the life of Stephen. His record moves us, too: remarkable layman of the Early Church; first martyr in the Christian family; the man whose spirit was so much like that of Christ our Lord. We'd like to be like Stephen if only there was some easy way to be like Stephen.

Let's think about him. Stephen was not among those first followers of Jesus known as the 12 disciples. But Acts 6 and 7 belong to him. If Matthias was significant because of his life of faithfulness, and Barnabas was significant because of his character of encouragement, then Stephen demands our attention because, above everything else, his life reflected the life of Christ our Lord. And we know in our hearts that ours should too, if only the price is not too high and the way too hard. Therefore we timidly ask the question, "How?" "How do we reflect Jesus?" Here is how Stephen did it.

I. STEPHEN REFLECTED CHRIST BECAUSE HE HAD GOD'S WORK IN HIS HANDS

That seems a simple and obvious truth to anyone sincerely intent on the beauty of Jesus. Stephen was busy about his Master's business. No wonder his Master was so evident in his life.

Acts 6:15 really deals with this. He appears on the Bible scene in Acts 6. In the growing body of faith there had arisen misunderstandings. Whether real or imagined, they were there. The Greek-speaking Hebrews felt that their needy people were getting less fair treatment than the Hebrew-speaking Hebrews. Maybe it was favoritism; maybe it was the language barrier; maybe it was just the feeling of being an outsider. But the need prompted the enlargement of the leadership roles of the Early Church.

Seven deacons were chosen by those early Christians. Their task was to distribute food to the needy. Their qualifications (v. 3) were to be recognized by all: wisdom and the fullness of the Spirit; common sense and clean hearts. Stephen was one of those selected. In fact, he is the first named.

We do not know where he came from; we do not know when he became a believer and a follower of Jesus. All we know is that in the brief history of the Early Church, Stephen had emerged as a responsible, spiritual man of God. He was, at that point, already so involved in the things of God that he was first choice for a particular task in the church of God. He had God's work in his hands.

God's work . . . waiting tables? Yes, God's work . . . waiting tables! When the average man thinks of God's work or God's workers he tends to think of the prominent leaders and the prominent leadership roles, the Billy Grahams and the Charles Swindolls and the James Dobsons. Or perhaps it is the pastor, or a staff person. But we must be careful not to define God's workers or God's work too narrowly. God's work is wherever God's people are, with a vision of doing and a willingness of being.

Stephen did his lowly task with such a spirit of godliness that God used him to accomplish "great wonders and miracles among the people" (v. 8). What wonders? What miracles? God saw no need to let us know that. He simply wanted us to know that it is being busy about His business that matters. The spectacular miracles are not necessarily more significant than daily toil. What matters is that whether toil or miracles, we are in the will of God doing the work of God.

Let's face it. Want to reflect Jesus the Lord? Then get involved in the work of the Lord. Let it grip you, possess you, challenge you, move you, measure you, and stretch you till you know you cannot do it on your own and that you need Him. And somehow others will begin to see Him in you.

II. Stephen Reflected Christ Because He Had God's Word in His Mind

In the synagogue of the Jews who had once been enslaved (v. 9), but who had earned or been granted freedom, Stephen shared his understanding of the Old Testament scripture—its promise of a Messiah and its call for repentance. His message was clear and powerful, but its conviction was troubling. His audience accused Stephen of blasphemy (v. 11) and called the Sanhedrin together where the charge was repeated because that Spirit-filled layman preached Jesus.

Before the Sanhedrin, the court that had condemned Jesus, Stephen spoke. Chapter 7 is his statement. It was a summary of the Old Testament—of God's call to men—of the few who listened and the many who ignored. Stephen spoke of those who heard God say, "Get up, get going, trust Me," and obeyed Him. That included Abraham, Joseph, and Moses; they listened and obeyed. He spoke of the people around them who wouldn't listen, much less obey. His conclusion of his own time focused on Jesus the Righteous One (7:52). He came to rescue, but He was betrayed and murdered. Stephen said it was the same old story repeated once more with tragic consequences.

Not a bad sermon for a layman. Not a bad sermon for anyone, for it was a message, born of the Word of God, that had taken root in the heart of Stephen. He believed it because it had done its work in him. I remember hearing a testimony one Sunday from Blaine Ashley, father of veteran missionary Bob Ashley. He said, "People ask me why I believe the Bible. I believe the Bible because of what I see it do in the lives of those who believe it and live it, and what I see it doesn't do in the lives of those who don't believe it and live it."

God's Word is alive and powerful. It is the seed of the gospel. There is life in the Word. It will bear fruit if we plant it, nurture it, and allow it to do its work. But life is busy and like the parable of the sower, the Word of God is confronted with hard ground, time pressures, and a multitude of things that would bug us to death and choke the Word of life (Matt. 13:3-9). Stephen reflected Christ because the Word of God was in his mind; it was at work in him. If it had not been, we would never have heard from him. We are what we feed on.

III. STEPHEN REFLECTED CHRIST BECAUSE HE HAD GOD'S SPIRIT IN HIS HEART

That was what set Stephen apart in the first place (Acts 6:3, 5). People identified him as "Spirit-filled"—a quality of life that reflected a relationship with God that was real, warm, and whole. Jesus had done a work in his life that had, by the Holy Spirit, written the law of God on his heart (Heb. 8:10). Stephen testified in life to a grace that both justifies freely and sanctifies wholly. It was a tribute that was twice repeated of him in his brief ministry of grace (6:5; 7:55).

Little wonder that there was something different about the look on his face (6:15). Little wonder that there was something different about the words on his lips as jagged boulders crushed life from him and an angry mob killed him. Only someone much like Jesus could say, would say, "Lord, lay not this sin to their charge" (7:60). How else can one explain it? Beyond God's work in his hand and God's word in his mind, Stephen knew the Spirit of God in his heart, cleansing him from rebellion against God and bitterness toward man.

There is a shallow kind of religion that, whatever its motivation, wants to *seem* spiritual. There is a genuine quality of religion that, above everything else, wants to *be* spiritual. There is a world of difference between them. Stephen had long since passed the shallows of only wanting to seem Christian. He had touched the deep wells of walking in the Spirit till that was both what he knew and what he wanted.

No wonder Stephen reflected Christ the Lord. The Spirit

of Jesus had been invited to make His home in Stephen's heart. And He did. He wants to do the same for all of us.

What a prayer there is for every child of God in the old hymn:

> *Breathe on me, breath of God,*
> *Fill me with life anew,*
> *That I may love what Thou dost love,*
> *And do what Thou wouldst do.*
>
> *Breathe on me, breath of God,*
> *Until my heart is pure,*
> *Until with Thee I will one will,*
> *To do and to endure.*
>
> *Breathe on me, breath of God,*
> *Till I am wholly thine,*
> *Until this earthly part of me*
> *Glows with Thy fire divine.*
>
> —EDWIN HATCH

4

Philip: Good News
Too Good to Keep

Acts 8:1–40

Have you ever noticed how natural it is for people, young or old, men or women, to talk about something new, whether a new thing or a new experience?

I pulled into our driveway one moonlit summer evening and was startled by the silhouette of a large bird in the top of the old digger pine below the driveway. He flopped his wings to another branch and serenaded the night with a few hoots. I rushed to the house to lead my wife and family out to witness that moment of nature—until the owl lumbered slowly away into the darkness. There is nothing new about owls, but that was the first one we had seen where we live in some 13 years. That made it conversation-topic number one for a few days.

We talk. We talk about new things, big things, little things, old things, trivial things, essential things. The plain fact is we love to talk.

So why is it that when it comes to the most important thing in the world, the good news of redemption in Jesus, that lockjaw seems to set in? Is it because religion is a private affair and you just don't trespass in that "no trespassing" zone of a person's life? Or is it because that is where the great spiritual battle goes on and somehow it is a battle we are not ready for?

But consider Philip, the early Christian for whom the Good News was too good to keep. In our roster of second-string heroes, first-class saints, we want to include Philip, who talks to us about talking to others for Jesus Christ. He really was a witness; he took the Good News and gave it away, with glory!

I. THE MAN

As is true with so many of the people of God we are looking at in this series, we know very little about Philip before he emerges on the stage of Christian history. To begin with, this is not Philip, the disciple, one of the Twelve whom Jesus called in the city of Bethsaida, the hometown of Peter and Andrew. This Philip first confronts us in Acts 6:5 as one of the seven Spirit-filled deacons selected by the Early Church to help distribute food to the needy believers. Where he came from we don't know. How he came to Jesus we don't know.

We first discover him in Jerusalem in Acts 6. Chapter 8, which belongs to Philip, finds him in ministry first in Samaria and then on the desert road to Egypt, ending in the coastal city of Caesarea. There is the note in 21:8 from the journey of Paul that he stayed, some 20 years later, in Caesarea at the home of Philip. The passage mentions that Philip had four daughters. So evidently it was in Caesarea that Philip settled down, made his home, and shared his faith.

But the interesting thing is that in Acts 21:8 Philip is called Philip the evangelist. He is the only person in the whole New Testament of whom the term is personally used. *Evangelist*— bearer of Good News. Philip's whole life was sharing the Good News. If we had written the Book of Acts, we would likely have given the title of evangelist to Paul, or perhaps Peter. But the Early Church saw in this layman named Philip the burden to bring others to Jesus. They knew him as a true evangelist because for him the Good News was too good to keep.

II. THE MINISTRY

There are two distinct segments to the ministry of Philip as we read it in Acts 8.

First, there is what we might call *public* evangelism, or mass evangelism (vv. 1-25). The persecution of Christians following the murder of Stephen drove all of them except the apostles from Jersualem. It seemed like a dark day for the work of Jesus. But in the continuing miracle of providence it became a good day. God used that circumstance to spread the seeds of faith and life. He had told them to go, and they did not. So He allowed the pressure to help them go. Behold the providential workings of God!

So Philip went north to Samaria, to people of mixed blood and mixed-up religion, part Jew and part pagan, with their own temple and their own holy place (John 4 tells us more). There were bad feelings between Jew and Samaritan. They did not socialize in any way. But don't tell that to Philip. He went there, and he went there to give himself away. Verse 5 states that he "preached Christ" to them and shared the fulfillment of the promise of the Messiah. He walked among them with the touch of a holy life. God used him: miracles took place. The sick were healed, and the possessed were set free. They abandoned their own witch doctor and both men and women believed in Jesus. Even the local witch doctor seemed to take the name of Jesus.

When word returned to the disciples in Jerusalem, Peter and John were sent north to check it out. They saw the need for a deepening of commitment and cleansing and therefore preached the promise of the Spirit-filled life. Verse 17 says they possessed that promise. Beyond the birth of the Spirit is the fullness of the Spirit. Beyond justification is entire sanctification.

It was the overflow of the Christian witness of Philip that took the gospel where it had never been, to a people that others would have counted out. Peter and John caught the vision from Philip, for on their return to Jerusalem (v. 25) they preached to the Samaritans too.

Second, there is what we would call *personal* evangelism, which is exemplified in the last half of Acts 8. The Lord directed Philip from Samaria southward about 100 miles to a desert road going toward Gaza. Philip, to his credit, went immediately on a mission he could not have fully understood, but it was an assignment he would not dismiss. You know the story—the chariot with the Ethiopian treasurer returning home from a worship pilgrimage to Jersualem. God moved Philip in classic personal evangelism style to open the conversation, to inquire if he understood the Bible he was reading, to climb into the chariot by invitation to preach Jesus to the man from Ethiopia. And out of that came personal faith and Christian baptism.

It was personal evangelism at its best, but our timid souls want to blurt out that it does not happen for us that way. Maybe it did not always happen that way for Philip. But it did that time, and it happened because he minded God and because he had developed a life-style of giving his faith away.

There is a *third* dimension of his ministry that I would term *private* evangelism. The clue is in Acts 21:8, concerning the visit of Paul some 20 years later to Philip's home in Caesarea. Paul stayed with Philip and his four daughters who are identified as having the gift of prophecy. This tells us that what Philip was in public, he was also in private, at home. While Philip was winning others to the Lord, he was also demonstrating faith and life at home with balance and warmth and winsomeness that brought his children into the family of God.

Don't miss that truth about Philip. What good is it if while winning the world to Jesus, we lose our own? While every person in every family is free to choose, and that choice can trample even the most blessed example, yet the greatest desire of every Christian is to see his own family established in Christ. There is no more noble prayer that can pass through the lips of men than this, "Lord, save my family." Philip, who won others to Christ, sought also to win his own and he did.

Mass or public evangelism; personal evangelism; private or family evangelism. No wonder they called him, this second-string layman—the evangelist.

III. THE MESSAGE

Jesus said his people would be witnesses to Him everywhere (Acts 1:8). In essence Jesus said that a Christian is one who helps make others Christian. But the haunting question of the soul is, Do we? Are we? If there are two areas where the majority of Christians struggle, it is in their life of prayer and their life of witnessing. We mean well; too often we fail miserably.

I have wondered why we fail to witness as we know we should and would suggest six reasons.

1. Some do not witness for Jesus because they do not know Him. One cannot tell another what he himself does not personally know any more than one can come back from a place he has never been. There are multitudes who have taken the name of Christ but who do not know Christ personally and therefore have nothing to say.

2. Some do not witness because even though they know Jesus, they do not know that they should share Jesus. There is the idea that it is the job of the professionals, the task of the trained ministry. But Acts 1:8 says it is everybody's assignment, and Philip's life is all the more dynamic because he was a layman.

3. There are those who do not witness because while they know Jesus and know that they should witness, in their lives there is such discouragement, turmoil, and defeat that they feel

totally unqualified to tell anyone how good it is to belong to Jesus. More than we want to admit, our outward witness for Christ is tied to our inward victory in Christ.

4. Some do not witness because they do not know how. "How do I share my faith, how do I overcome objections, how do I clarify the issues, how do I help someone put his trust in Christ and not his own works?" I believe that there is a new wind in the church equipping believers to share their faith. There is a new awareness that the role of ministry is to equip believers for their ministry (Eph. 4:12, NIV). Nothing more vital could happen in the church than a laity prepared and motivated to share their faith.

5. There is a group who do not witness because they have tried and failed, and it is hard to try again. Nobody likes to reach out and be slapped down, to love and be rejected. There is no clause, however, in Acts 1:8 that exempts even the wounded from telling the Good News.

6. Some do not witness simply because they do not care enough to do it. In the busyness of life, and the demands of living, building relationships for the purpose of faith-sharing is given a low priority. It is easier to tithe than it is to care about the lost souls of men.

But for all the reasons why many don't, there is the great example of Philip who did! It strikes me as interesting that the name Philip means "lover of horses." The truth is that Philip was a lover of men, and he wanted with all his heart to see them come to the Savior. Small wonder, then, that they did.

Oh, that the spirit of Philip might rest upon us.

5

Cornelius:
Daring to Go Deeper

Acts 10:1–48; 15:8–9

A few years ago, a Wall Street lawyer with a background of both fundamental Christianity and Yale Divinity School, went on the Phil Donahue program to announce, "There is a way out of fundamentalism." Thirty-year-old Richard Yao is the founder of a group called Fundamentalists Anonymous, an organization that now sends out its newsletter to some 17,000 people and at last count had some 31 chapters nationwide.

The major premise of Fundamentalists Anonymous is that fundamental Christianity can be hazardous to your health, can leave a trail of wrecked lives, shattered minds, and scarred personalities—can push some people over the edge.[1]

This is of interest to me. When properly defined, my church is conservative. Both in theology and practice, we believe in the fundamentals of the biblical faith. In the eyes of those who want what Fundamentalists Anonymous offers, we are what they *don't want*. FA says it exists to help people find their way out of the devastation of a personal relationship with God through Jesus Christ. But as I look at the vital and vibrant lives of dedicated and Spirit-filled Christians whom I know, I have to believe that FA is either talking about somebody else or simply wanting what the natural man has always wanted, that is, that God would leave him alone.

The man named Cornelius would have had no use for a chapter of Fundamentalists Anonymous in his town. The deep hunger of his life was not for less of God but for more of God—a walk with Him that was deep, clean, wholesome, and redemptive. What Cornelius sought, he found.

Let's add him to our list of God's second-string heroes, first-class saints. He, like the others in this list from the Book of Acts, has a unique focus. Cornelius speaks to us about daring to go deeper. Acts 10 belongs to him.

I. DESIRING GOD'S BEST

Cornelius comes out of nowhere, and beyond chap. 10 is heard from no more, save the single historical reference of Peter in chap. 15. The life of Cornelius, however, is vital in Christian history, both for what God did through him and for what God did in him.

Cornelius was a Roman soldier, likely Italian with the heritage of Rome itself. As a professional soldier he had risen through the ranks to become an officer in charge of 100 soldiers garrisoned in Caesarea, the coastal city that served as Rome's provincial capital of Judea. In the eyes of the world, Cornelius was a somebody. Julian the Apostate reckoned him as one of the few persons of distinction of that time who became a Christian.

His character, described in verses 2-4, is that of a man of deep religious inclination. While he was not a full convert to the Jewish religion, he was one who saw in Jewish monotheism the appeal of purity, integrity, compassion, and spirituality. Roman paganism and polytheism had long since lost all appeal for Cornelius. He longed for something more. He belonged to that company of great souls of all times who lived above their creeds. He had a "homesickness for holiness." He prayed daily and fervently. He helped others. He feared God. Those who

33

knew him best called him "a just man." He walked in the light he had till God gave him the light he longed for.

Little wonder, then, that Cornelius was a person of influence upon others for God. People may not be impressed by what we say, but they are impressed by what we are. Verse 2 says his whole house shared his piety; verse 7 mentions at least one of his soldiers as a man of devotion. Nobody walks through life in isolation. Either we lift those around us or we drag them down. Cornelius was a balcony person, a lifter of men.

Cornelius is signficant. God chose him to be the first of the Gentiles to come through the front doors of the Christian invitation to all men to find life eternal in Jesus Christ. The spiritual heritage of Christians like us goes back to the spiritual experience of that Gentile named Cornelius.

But the moving force in the life of Cornelius was his hunger for God—his deep noble desire to be all that God wanted him to be, to do all that God wanted him to do, to know God in a deep and life-satisfying way. His life said that; his prayers said that; his troops and friends knew that. It was no secret.

It was A. W. Tozer who noted that "to most people God is an inference, not a reality. He is a deduction from evidence which they consider adequate; but He remains personally unknown to the individual."[2] It was the burden of his message to encourage modern Christians to follow hard after God like deep souls always have. In that company was Cornelius, who had the armor of a soldier but a heart for God.

II. DISCOVERING GOD'S BEST

The record of verses 3-4 indicates that one afternoon in prayer God broke in upon Cornelius, and Cornelius broke through to God's new way.

The story is long. Instructions from a "holy angel" were given to send men to Joppa 30 miles away for the purpose of bringing back a man called Simon Peter. The instructions also included specific information as to where this man could be found in that city. Cornelius sent his servants immediately.

In Joppa, God was preparing Peter for this crucial encounter during a noon prayer time and a vision of a sheet full of animals. This vision and the messengers' invitation prompted Peter to understand that God was doing a new thing. Outsiders were no longer to be considered as outsiders.

Peter went with the men the next day to the house of Cornelius and preached the message of Jesus Christ (vv. 34-43). It involved His life, ministry, deity, death, resurrection—the testimony of Scripture, the offer of forgiveness and life in Him. Our message is Jesus. Take away, that and we have nothing to say.

The message of Christ proclaimed led to the person of Christ experienced, for as Peter came to the conclusion of his address, the Holy Spirit was poured out upon the hungry soldier and his gathering of friends and servants. God came. Something happened. Heaven and earth touched. God and man met. Life would never be the same again.

Even though Cornelius is not heard from again in the record of Scripture, I have to believe that he who was a sincere seeker and became a genuine finder, went on to become a faithful witness of the Christ who came and made all things new. Those who seek Him find Him. Said Jeremiah, "And ye shall seek me, and find me, when ye shall search for me with all your heart" (Jer. 29:13).

The call of the gospel is an invitation to have one's own experience of saving, sanctifying grace. God waits to be wanted. Too bad that with so many He waits so long, so very long, in vain.

III. DEFINING GOD'S BEST

While Cornelius is not specifically mentioned again, the event in his house is referred to a few years later during the council meeting in Jerusalem. The basic issue centered around the all-encompassing message of the gospel and its relation to the Gentiles. In the midst of the discussion Peter arose to remind them that God had settled that issue earlier in the experience of Cornelius. In his own words, Peter recreated the scene at the house in Caesarea: "And God, which knoweth the hearts, bare them witness, giving them the Holy Ghost, even as he did unto us; and put no difference between us and them, purifying their hearts by faith" (Acts 15:8-9). What happened was what always happens when God does His best work in human life.

Peter made three basic statements.

First, God knows the heart. Jeremiah once said, "The heart is deceitful above all things, and desperately wicked: who can know it?" (Jer. 17:9). The answer to the question is that God can and does. Nothing is hidden from Him. He knows the shame of it, and He knows the sincerity of it. And God responds to the heart He knows—with conviction for sin and comfort for obedience. God knew the heart of Cornelius. This heart possessed a hunger for holiness that God moved to meet.

Second, God cleanses the heart. The human heart that is so polluted He proposes to make new, to make clean, and to make His. It is the promise of the Word of God, and it is the witness of the life of the people of God.

It is a glorious thing to be forgiven. Those who are truly penitent know that. It means that the charges are not only dropped but also eliminated from the record. The intention of redemption, however, is more than forgiveness. It is cleansing. It is the good law of God once again inscribed on the heart of man, restoring him both to peace with God and to peace with himself. Some dramatic things happened on the Day of Pentecost. Some of those things were repeated at the house of Cornelius. But what Peter singled out as permanently significant was the inward event of God cleansing the heart.

Third, God enters the heart. Verse 8 states it: "Giving them the Holy Ghost, even as he did unto us." The Holy Spirit is the Spirit of Jesus, God with us. Dr. D. Shelby Corlett called Him, "God in the present tense."[3] When we open ourselves to Him, He comes into us. He begins in the birth of the Spirit with a quickening. But in response to our full yielding, He comes with a fullness of the Spirit. If God cleansed but did not fill what He cleansed, then in emptiness it would quickly be filthy again. But when God cleanses, it is in order that He himself may make His home in our hearts.

> It is by grace—for He does for us what we cannot do for ourselves.
>
> It is by faith—for the Holy Spirit is not a prize to be won but a Gift to be received.
>
> It is for all—all men, all time, all ages.

Cornelius went deeper. The call is for us to do the same.

6

Mark:
One Strike Is Not Out

Acts 12:12; 13:5, 13; 15:36–39

Some of the best advice I ever heard came from Dr. H. Orton Wiley in a chapel service at Pasadena College. This gifted theologian, pioneer leader in the church, and then president of the college said: "If perhaps someday you do something very, very good and your heart is puffed with pride, it is a good thing to bring it to the Lord, and forget it, and go on your way in Him. And, if perhaps someday you do something very foolish and your heart is heavy with condemnation, it is a good thing to bring it to the Lord, and forget it, and go on your way in Him."

It is not a new thought. But it is a great thought. Perhaps as you watched the tennis matches of Wimbledon you saw the lines of Kipling chiseled in the entrance to the London Tennis Club at Wimbledon: "If you can meet with Triumph and Disaster / And treat those two impostors just the same . . . "

Then Kipling went on to say,

> Yours is the Earth and everything that's in it,
> And—which is more—you'll be a Man, my son![1]

That is something we learn from the life of the man we know as Mark. John Mark is his Bible name. He is another of God's second-string heroes who became by the grace of God a first-class saint. If Matthias speaks to us about faithfulness, Barnabas about encouragement, Stephen about godliness, Philip about witnessing, Cornelius about Spirit-fullness, then Mark speaks about perseverance in God's great grace, turning defeat into victory and foolishness into godliness. In the language of baseball, "One strike is not out." In the language of the soul, "If you fall, fall to your knees, and then get up and get going." That is the reason we remember Mark more than 1900 years later.

I. Early in His Life Mark Got In

We remember him because early in his life Mark got in— he became a Christian, he gave his heart to Jesus. He became a significant member of the Body of Christ, but then every believer is a significant member of the Body of Christ.

Mark had a Christian heritage that he did not despise but treasured. He made it his own. What we know is just a little, but it all helps to put the story together. Acts 12:12 tells of the time of Peter's imprisonment by Herod and his scheduled execution. Peter, like James, was a pawn in the game of politics. The body of believers went to prayer that God would spare Peter, even though for reasons we will never know God had not spared James (v. 2).

And God did. In a miracle of deliverance Peter was free. Immediately he set out to find his people. He knew where they would be . . . at Mark's home, or better at the home of Mark's mother (12:12). That is where a prayer meeting of power was going on.

That is the kind of holy heritage Mark had. Earlier, his mother had become a Christian. Her home in Jerusalem was headquarters for the Church of Christ. While Mark's father is not mentioned, and therefore was likely deceased, the family was evidently well-to-do. Their home was large enough for that prayer gathering, and the family was able to afford at least one servant girl named Rhoda (12:13). It is possible that this is the home where the Last Supper was held; this is the home where the 120 prayed and the Holy Spirit came on the Day of Pentecost. It is likely that the young boy who followed Jesus and the disciples from the Upper Room to Gethsemane and observed the arrest of Jesus was Mark himself. Only his Gospel tells the incident, something that no one but an eyewitness would have known (Mark 14:51-52).

Even with that kind of background, Mark still had to come to commitment to Christ personally. God has no grandchildren, only children, who by their own faith and commitment are born of the Spirit and adopted into the family of God. It is likely that Peter was the one who led Mark to a commitment to Jesus, for Peter calls him his son (1 Pet. 5:13).

The faith of his mother was significant. The commitment of his uncle or cousin Barnabas was influential too. But all of that would have been nothing if Mark had not for himself said, "I choose Jesus. I want my heart to be His home. I will be His, now and forever."

Sometimes young people who are born into Christian homes struggle hard to find themselves. There can be strong impulses to rebel and pull away and deny their family and faith in order to be themselves. Sometimes there is such comfort in a great family heritage that they just stay with it, assuming it is all theirs by inheritance, and never personally make it their own.

Both extremes miss the point. Thank God for the Christian heritage if you have it. Don't deny it, but don't take it for granted either. God wants you to have your own experience of grace. Get in, really in. Mark did, and so can you.

II. LATER IN HIS LIFE MARK CUT OUT

He went so far and then stopped. Mark became a classic quitter. Acts 13 is the record of the first missionary journey of the Christian church. Its leaders were Barnabas and Paul, in that order. It started in Antioch of Syria, then went to the coast and later to the island of Cyprus, the home of Barnabas. It was around A.D. 46 that Mark, who was probably in his early 20s, was asked by his esteemed uncle Barnabas to go along as their helper in ministry.

What an opportunity for a young Christian—on the cutting edge of the movement of God, in the company of the greatest of the great. What a school for godliness.

But Mark blew it. He quit and went home, not just back to Antioch but back to Jerusalem (Acts 13:13). Nobody knows for sure why. Some think Mark was offended as Paul emerged as leader over Barnabas. Some think that Jerusalem-reared and orthodox-conservative Mark had a hard time with the gospel being shared with Gentiles. Some think he became homesick and followed his heart back home.

Whatever the reason, Mark cut out. For seven years nothing is heard of him. When the second missionary journey was ready for launching, Barnabas wanted Mark, his nephew, now seven years older, to travel with them again, but Paul would have no part of that. The controversy was so great that Paul and Barnabas parted over it. Paul took Silas. Barnabas, true to his character of encouragement, invited Mark to be his companion in ministry.

It was stupid, what Mark did. Whatever his reasons or reasoning, he really blew it when he quit.

Why do we do stupid things? That is the question. Why do we walk tall one day and then fall flat on our faces the next? The gifted A. W. Tozer once wrote an editorial titled "To Be Right, We Must Think Right."[2] His premise was that our thoughts predict our actions, and that behind any foolish action is some pretty stupid thinking. And on the positive side, behind any noble action is some pretty godly thinking.

Tozer was right. Think stupid and you will act stupid every time. Follow the devil's logic and you will buy the devil's lie. And for Mark, whether it was his pride (loyalty to Barnabas against Paul) or his prejudice (against the Gentiles receiving the gospel), the thinking was unwise and was not God's but his own.

No wonder the Bible again and again admonishes us to get quiet before God and think about high and holy things as a preliminary to any good deed or courageous act. No wonder after Paul listed the virtues of the faith, he said, "Think on these things" (Phil. 4:8).

Mark went home. Nobody stopped him. But I think that for most of those seven years, there was an ache in his soul that yearned for a chance to do it over again—and this time so much better.

III. LATER ON MARK CAME BACK

That is why we remember him. The record does not end with Acts 13:13. Seven years later God opened the door of providence again. The sting of Paul's rejection must have been painful to Mark, even though it may have been justified. But the vote of confidence from Barnabas was an encouragement he would not pass up (15:36-39). Off they headed in ministry—off to a new start and a second chance.

And while Acts makes no more mention of Mark, the Bible can't forget him. In less than 10 years Paul would be writing to Timothy saying, "Get Mark and bring him with you, because he is helpful to me in my ministry" (2 Tim. 4:11, NIV). And Paul writing to the Colossians asked them to receive Mark warmly if he was able to come their way (Col. 4:10). Peter, before he left this world, noted in closing his first letter that Mark was with him and sent greetings (1 Pet. 5:13).

When you open your New Testament you have not turned many pages until you come to the Gospel that bears his name.

Scholars tell us that it was the first of the Gospels to be written; that Mark gathered it from his association with Peter; that it was written to the Roman world, dynamic and convincing.

Tradition tells us that Mark went to Alexandria, started the church there, and eventually died for his Lord in the persecution by Nero.

Not a bad record for a young man who on a bad day on Cyprus said, "I quit," only to realize that he goofed. By the grace of God he arose and restarted.

That is the good news always. It says if you are down you do not have to stay down. As Dr. Wiley said, "Give it to God and get going again."

One strike is not out. Jesus is in the special business of giving new starts to folk who made a mess of previous opportunities.

7

Timothy:
Making the Most of It

Acts 16:1-3

When we talk about "making the most," ears open wide. Our culture now, as has been true of cultures of all times, has a remarkable fascination with the details of people at the top. A recent magazine article cataloged the top wage earners of 1987. (We have no secrets from the IRS.) The top executive of the year was Lee Iacocca of Chrysler Corporation who came close to grossing $21 million for the year with stock options included, far surpassing other top executives who cashed in at about $5 million each.

The big-buck earners, however, were the entertainers. Entertainment is big business, whatever that may say about our world. With our soaring trade deficit and the national dilemmas it poses, it is interesting to note that entertainment is our second largest producer of trade surplus, outranked only by aircraft. Bill Cosby topped the chart with a tidy $57 million, followed by singer Michael Jackson at $31 million and cartoonist Charles Schulz at $30 million. They're the guys who made the most. Not everybody can do that.[1]

But everybody can "make the most of it"—take life and its opportunities, possibilities, abilities and manage them to their high potential. That's what I think of when I read of Timothy.

We know as much about him as any other person in the New Testament with the exceptions of Paul and Peter. His record is a noble one. Timothy is to my mind the New Testament ideal of youth, even as Joseph and Daniel were the Old Testament ideal of youth. He, like they, came on the scene with high goals and lofty purpose and never gave up. In short, he made the most of it.

Timothy should be added to our list of second-string heroes who did indeed become one of the choice saints of God.

I. TIMOTHY HAD A HOLY HERITAGE AND HE HONORED IT

The clues to the life of Timothy are hinted at throughout the pages of Acts and the Epistles. Acts 16:1 informs us that his mother was Jewish and his father was Greek. More is communicated by 2 Tim. 1:5 where Paul speaks of the Christian faith "which dwelt first in thy grandmother Lois, and thy mother Eunice; and I am persuaded that in thee also." Paul also notes in 3:15 that Timothy had from childhood "known the holy scriptures, which are able to make thee wise unto salvation through faith which is in Christ Jesus."

During the first missionary journey, Paul and Barnabus arrived at a place called Lystra in Asia Minor (Acts 14:6 ff.) where they preached the gospel with both success and frustration. Some tried to crown the two missionaries as gods; troublemakers came and stoned Paul to the point they believed he was dead (v. 19). Recovering, the team left, preached the gospel in other places, came back through to establish the new converts, and then returned to Jerusalem.

A few years later, Paul and Silas returned to Lystra and preached again where Paul had labored before. That point marked the entry of Timothy into the pages of sacred history (16:1 ff.). My assumption is that on Paul's first ministry in Lystra, his message of Christ the Messiah found its target in the hearts of Lois and Eunice, devout Jewish women who wanted to be all that God wanted them to be. Their knowledge of the Old Testament scriptures became the soil of their commitment to Christ. The husband of Eunice did not join her in commitment, but neither do we read of any interference from him.

Faith is a family matter. Children tend to copy parents. Christian parents are God's best preachers. Somewhere in that first ministry in Lystra, Timothy also gave his heart to the Lord Jesus. Later Paul called Timothy "my own son in the faith" (1 Tim. 1:2) and "my dearly beloved son" (2 Tim. 1:2).

How old was Timothy when he gave his heart to the Lord? The Bible does not say. I will guess he was about 14. That would mean he was about 19 when Paul returned (Acts 16:1); maybe 30 years old when Paul wrote his first letter to Timothy and said, "Let no man despise thy youth" (1 Tim. 4:12); perhaps 33 when Paul asked Timothy to hurry to Rome to be with him in those last days before execution (2 Tim. 4:9, 21).

So Timothy most likely came to Christ in his early teens. That speaks to me. The gospel door of eternal life is open to people of all ages, and we are thankful for that. But young years are God's best years. He can do His best with a whole life, a clean life.

I like Timothy because he made the most of the godly heritage that was his. It would have been better if his dad had come to faith also. There is no mention of brothers and sisters, but if there were, their sharing the faith would have enriched the family relationships even more.

God gave Timothy enough gospel light for him to understand, and he responded, "I choose Jesus." How marvelous it would be if every young person would honor the holy heritage that has pointed his soul heavenward!

If you have a Christian heritage, then thank God for it. It is worth more than silver or gold. If you have a mother or father who have walked with Jesus before you, be grateful and follow also. If you have or have had a parent who has invested years in the church and the spiritual lives of people, be glad and make the most of that heritage. That is what Timothy did, and we honor him for it nearly 20 centuries later.

II. Timothy Had a Great Opportunity and He Accepted It

Paul was impressed by Timothy. Everybody spoke well of him, both in his home area of Lystra and as far away as Iconium, some 20 miles distant. Evidently he possessed the gifts and graces, the personality and character, the discipline and the wisdom that built bridges of confidence and respect.

Acts 16:3 simply says, "Him would Paul have to go forth with him." And Timothy went. He did not have to go. As a 19-year-old he could have stayed in Lystra, could have closed the door of opportunity for Christian service. God does not say that everybody has to take distant journeys to honor Him. But God does call His people to serve Him, to touch our world for Him in the ways we can. Timothy did. When that significant opportunity for Christian service opened he grabbed it.

It was some 10 years later that Paul wrote his first letter to Timothy in Ephesus where the young Christian was overseeing the work of the believers in that area. Across those intervening years Timothy had been with Paul in a host of places—Philippi, Thessalonica, Berea, Corinth. He had gone on special assignments for him—to Thessalonica (1 Thess. 3:2) and to Philippi (Phil. 2:19).

That willingness to serve, to accept an opportunity for Christian service, made some tough demands on Timothy. To our knowledge he did not face the intensity of persecution that Paul encountered, but there is the note in Heb. 13:23 "that our brother Timothy is set at liberty" (*The Living Bible* says, "out of

47

jail"). There was a cost to discipleship for Timothy, just as there is for everyone. God's grace is free, but never cheap. But that obedience was bestowing a benefit worth more than money. In following Jesus, Timothy was becoming more like Jesus. The apostle Paul tutored him and discipled him, challenging Timothy to be "an example of the believers, in word, in conversation, in charity, in spirit, in faith, in purity" (1 Tim. 4:12). Paul said it because it was happening.

Do you want to grow as a Christian? Then accept the opportunities of service that God brings across your path. Make the most of them. There is in our culture an ingrained disposition to leisure, to play. It is not all wrong, but it can be far from what God is wanting and willing. Jesus talked about looking on the fields and seeing what He sees, fields ready for harvest, praying for laborers for that harvest (John 4:35 ff.).

The question becomes, "What are you doing with your opportunities for Christian witness, for Christian love, for Christian growth, for Christian service?" Timothy had a great opportunity for Christian service and he accepted it—made the most of it.

III. TIMOTHY HAD A SIGNIFICANT ASSIGNMENT AND HE FULFILLED IT

Evidently the opportunity for Christian service became the avenue by which God clarified His call to Timothy to Christian ministry. He was more than a flunky; he was an emerging shepherd of the flock. By the time he was about 30, he was the pastor of the Christian community in the strategic city of Ephesus, preaching Jesus Christ, opening the Scripture, defending the faith, building the church, training workers, winning souls.

Some think that Timothy had some character weaknesses. Paul talked about his timidity and his tendency to tears (2 Tim.

1:4, 7). He challenged the young preacher to "stir up the gift of God, which is in thee by the putting on of my hands" (v. 6). He reminded him that bodily exercise had some benefits, but not as much as godliness (1 Tim. 4:8). He told him to study hard and to work faithfully (2 Tim. 2:15). He cautioned him about youthful lusts (v. 22) and counseled him about apparent stomach disorders (1 Tim. 5:23).

Perfect? Not in performance, perhaps, but his heart was right. God was at work in Timothy, so much so that the apostle Paul paid him the high tribute of telling the Christians at Philippi, "I have no man likeminded" (Phil. 2:20). (*The Living Bible* translates it: "There is no one like Timothy for having a real interest in you; everyone else seems to be worrying about his own plans and not those of Jesus Christ. But you know Timothy. He has been just like a son to me in helping me preach the Good News" [vv. 20-22].

And when the apostle knew that the end of his life was at hand, his last letter was to Timothy. The urgent request was for Timothy "to come before winter" (2 Tim. 4:21; see also v. 9).

The whole implication was that the mantle of Christian leadership was moving to younger shoulders, like Timothy, who under God made the most of the opportunity that was his.

I have great respect for Dr. Billy Graham. For more than 40 years he has been God's voice to man's world, a voice that has been used of God in multitudes of lives, including mine. Recently he reached his 70th birthday. In an earlier interview he indicated that while he was weary of the world's iniquities and ready to move on to heaven, he no longer talks about retiring. He said, "I've quit that because I feel so good." And so his crusade schedule is still full, and his plans for touching his world for Christ are still dynamic. Like Timothy before him, Graham is making the most of his opportunities.

How about you?

8

Lydia:
A Touch of Class

Acts 16:12–15, 40

When the Washington Redskins whipped the upstart Minnesota Vikings on their way to the 1988 National Football League Championship, they celebrated their victory in part by handing out T-shirts imprinted with a picture of quarterback Doug Williams and the tribute—"A Touch of Class." It was the team's way of saying thanks to their second-string quarterback who had taken over and done a job that not many ever expected.

"Class." It can have negative overtones such as snobby, fussy, self-centered, shallow, or pompous—none of which is good and all of which are offensive. But "class" can also be and should be positive—denoting a bearing, a discipline, a winsomeness that displays the best of life and brings out the best in life. It is perhaps another word in our vernacular for "grace"—life at its best. And if anybody should have class in that positive, attractive, winsome meaning, it should be the people of God. When one pastor friend of mine pays someone a compliment he says, "He's a class person."

I doubt that it has much to do with education, though education certainly ought not to hurt it. I doubt that it has anything to do with wealth as such, or fame, or position. Class is possible for anybody—and therefore everybody. If God has His way in us, then "class" should be inevitable. Ray Ortlund talked about the "elegance of godliness." The apostle Paul cataloged a litany of the "works of the flesh" (Gal. 5:19-21) and noted God's hatred of them. To read the list, from sexual immorality to vileness of spirit, is to be impressed by the fact that there is no "class" in sin. But Paul also celebrated the "fruit of the Spirit" (vv. 22-23), from love to self-control. And to contemplate that set of virtues is to sense indeed the surpassing beauty of holiness—"class" indeed.

When I think of Christians with that touch of class I think, among many, many others, of Lydia, the first recorded Christian convert of Europe. Everything I read about her impresses me that everything "class" is Lydia was.

I. CONSIDER LYDIA THE PERSON

Her whole story is told in Acts 16. We find her in Philippi, the Roman colony of Macedonia. We never heard of her before, nor shall we read of her again, but everything that is said of her is so compellingly good that we can do nothing but pay her honor.

First, we are told that she was from Thyatira, a city of western Asia Minor in a region that was called "Lydia." Somewhere, sometime, she had moved across the Bosporus into Europe, and in the strategic city of Philippi she operated a business that specialized in purple cloth. Her native city was famous for that purple dye, produced from a certain shellfish.

Just how successful a businesswoman Lydia was we are not told, but the home that she had would be adequate to entertain the four missionaries that she would meet, and the influence of her eventual conversion would carry her household into faith too—either family, employees, or slaves. That is class. Lydia had her act together. In a day when a woman's place was in the home, she found a place outside of the home, either by necessity or by choice, and she did it well.

Lydia was more than commercially successful, she was spiritually sensitive. Though a Gentile by birth, she had become a worshiper of Jehovah God (vv. 13-14). She had thrown aside the pagan superstition of Roman mythology, and the coarse ways so often associated with it, for the higher road of holy living embodied in the Jewish worship of God at its best. There were not many like her in Philippi. In fact there was not even a Jewish synagogue there, only a handful of Jewish women and/or Gentile women converts to the creed and code. The mention is that they gathered for prayer at a certain spot on the shore of Gangites River. The rule was that if there were 10 Jewish men in any community who wanted a synagogue, they must have one. Evidently there weren't. So the life of faith was nurtured by that ladies' prayer group meeting regularly together with the God they loved in order that they might live the life they believed He wanted.

It takes a lot to live above the crowd. Lydia did it. It takes a lot to hunger for holiness in an unholy world. Lydia wanted that. It takes a lot to be successful in the eyes of the world and humble in the eyes of God, but Lydia was all of that.

No wonder then that Lydia was the one the Holy Spirit moved to be the first Christian convert in the new missionary thrust of the gospel to the fertile soil of Europe. God does not limit His gospel call to gracious people. He loves us all, accepts us all, polishes us all. But let's not forget that He has a love for "class" people too. Lydia was one of them.

II. Consider Lydia the Convert

When Paul's missionary group discovered no synagogue in town but heard of a prayer meeting by the riverside, they made their way on the Sabbath day to join them and to teach the simple gospel of Jesus to the women gathered there. There is no record of the sermon given, nor any mention of the size of the group. There are no details except that Lydia's heart was opened by the Lord as she heard the saving message. Without doubt those missionaries talked about sin in the heart versus life in the Son; the saving power of Jesus Christ the Messiah, incarnate, crucified, risen, and coming again. No doubt they asked life's greatest questions, "Do you know Him personally?" and "Will you receive Him trustingly?" Lydia's heart warmed; it made sense to this lady who was trying hard to do right and be right. It fit with what she knew of Old Testament scripture and appealed to her soul that hungered after righteousness.

The story is told of two seminary students in the South who were out calling one afternoon when they came upon a run-down house with about a dozen kids yelling at play in an unkept yard. The seminary students made their way through the children toward the house where a weary and perspiring mother labored over a washboard. They greeted her and drove straight to their message, saying, "Lady, would you like to live forever?" She paused from her washing for a moment, looked at them, then at the boisterous children, then at the wash in front of her, and shook her head saying, "Right now I don't think I could stand it."

But Lydia said, "Yes. I want Jesus." As far as we know it was the first time she ever heard the Good News or listened to a call to Christian decision. She answered: "I take Him."

How many sermons does it take for the Lord to build a bridge to a person's heart? How many fellowships does it take to make a person feel like he wants to belong? How many hymns does it take to make a person think about eternal matters? It usually takes a while—weeks, months, or even years. But all it has to take is one time—one time when the heart is there, the hunger is there, the Lord is there, and the message is there.

Bo Cassell is a tall, intelligent, gifted young man now in seminary preparation for the Christian ministry. But nine years ago he was a high school freshman when his friend Kevin Monroe invited him to our church to hear the youth choir present their final concert from their brief tour. They sang; I gave a simple invitation and invited anyone present who wanted to know the Savior about whom the youth had sung to see me after the concert. The service was over; excited people greeted the choir and each other and left. There was Bo, too, saying politely, "I'd like to do what you invited me to do." So, on that first hearing of the Christian invitation to decision, we shared and prayed and Jesus came into his life with reality and power. One time, if it is God's time, is all the time we really need.

Lydia was like that. She believed and she was baptized. The water was there, and she obeyed her Lord in the waters of baptism. Members of her household who were there at the place of prayer joined her in her step of discipleship, a tribute to her integrity and strength.

Acts 16 is a case study in Christian conversions. Three are either described or referred to here. One is Timothy who came to Christ as a young teen out of the holy heritage from his mother and grandmother who taught him the Old Testament scriptures (2 Tim. 3:15) and who came to Christ themselves before Timothy did (1:5). It was a conversion like a sunrise, quiet but real. The second is that of the Philippian jailer (Acts 16:27-34), the tough cop of the world who could be as brutal as necessary. He was ready to take his own life for letting his prisoners escape (he thought). Instead he was compelled to faith by the remarkable actions of Paul and Silas who saved his life not only by their refusal to escape but also by their willingness to witness. What a dramatic conversion, a complete turnaround, in a class along with others like Charles Colson, Pete Maravich, or the apostle Paul himself.

The third is that of Lydia—steady, gracious, quiet, but oh so real. The first convert of Europe; but what a model for others to come.

III. Consider Lydia the Christian

Her background, conversion, and the record of Lydia's Christian life are all compressed into these few words of Acts 16. What did she do once the Lord had "opened her heart"? Well, she did what people of faith have always done. She gave the Lord what she had. In Lydia's case that meant she opened her home to be headquarters for the missionary team of Paul, Silas, Luke, and Timothy. They were hesitant, but she "persuaded" them, and she did it as a service to her Lord (v. 15).

Her house became the first house church in Europe, and the Lord used her and her self-sacrifice for the advancing of the church. It was not necessarily convenient. It meant four more mouths to feed, accommodations to provide, interruptions to work around. Spiritual progress, however, is not made at the point of convenience but at the point of commitment.

Nor was this new arrangement necessarily easy. Paul and his friends soon became the focus of the unwanted attention of a demon-possessed slave girl who stuck to them like gum on a shoe. It went on "day after day" (v. 18, TLB). It ended with not only the healing of the girl but also the anger of her masters and the imprisonment of Paul and Silas. No house enjoys that kind of torment. The last specific mention of Lydia is in verse 40 when Paul and Silas, backs bloody from beatings, bodies weary from an incredible night, were released, and with hearts rejoicing in the conversion of the jailer, went back to the house of Lydia.

That last stay would be short, for they were under official orders to get out of town. But the memories would be lasting.

Later Paul would write back to people he said he "held in his heart" (see Phil. 1:7) and make a special request to "help those women which laboured with me in the gospel . . . whose names are in the book of life" (Phil. 4:3). It seems to me he must have been thinking of Lydia. It seems to me that she was likely among those who gave to his needs more than once (4:15-16). She did what she could, and she did it with class.

We can call it whatever we want: style, grace, winsomeness, attractiveness, propriety, wholesomeness . . .

We can call it the elegance of godliness . . .

We can call it the beauty of holiness . . .

We can call it Christian class . . .

We can call it the spirit of Jesus . . .

But whatever we call it, let us seek it, that "mind [in us], which was also in Christ Jesus" (Phil. 2:5) and which His Spirit is seeking to impart into the lives of those who would be His.

9

Silas:
When Life Holds More
than You Bargained For

Acts 16:26–34

Do you recall a time when you allowed someone to talk you into something? The pitch was presented and the appeal was so attractive that you went for it. Then something happened. Everything went sour—to such a degree that you wondered how you ever in your right mind consented to such a deal. You remember, then, saying over and over in Laurel and Hardy style, "Now just look what a fine mess you got us into!"

Who hasn't experienced such a collapse of bright expectations. Ater all, the "best laid plans of mice and men quite often go astray." For everybody who makes a million in investments, somebody loses. For every person who makes it to the top of the corporate ladder, multitudes plateau far below that. Everyone has a story to tell of what was supposed to happen that didn't quite turn out that way.

What do you do when life holds more—or less—than you bargained for? I think of that when I read about Silas. He is another of God's second-string heroes who became a first-class saint. Matthias, Barnabas, Stephen, Philip, Cornelius, Mark, Timothy, and Lydia all had their special strengths. To me, Silas models endurance—that trait of character that does not give up when things do not go as planned.

I. A Man of Bright Promise

Silas first enters the history of the church in Acts 15:22. The setting there centers in the return of Paul and Barnabas to Jerusalem after their first missionary journey. They tell with joy of the effective spread of the gospel, with even Gentiles accepting Christ and knowing the transforming power of personal faith in Jesus. While many were excited about this startling expansion of the faith, others were troubled. Somebody said once, "The seven last words of a dying church are: 'we never did it that way before.'"

So the conflict called for a meeting. James, the brother of our Lord, presided. Peter spoke for an open policy, citing what happened with Cornelius and God's evident revelation to Peter of the validity of Gentile ministry. The Christian Pharisees made their case that the only way to be a Christian was to be a Jew. Paul and Barnabas told about the work of God among the Gentiles. The Early Church had to come to a crucial decision—the gospel was for the Gentiles, too, with the only considerations beyond saving faith in Christ being (1) moral purity; (2) spiritual consistency; and (3) cultural distinctiveness (15:20, 28-29).

With that agreement reached, they selected two men to go with Paul and Barnabas to certify the ruling of the council to the distant outpost of the church in Antioch. The men chosen were Judas Barsabas and Silas, who were known as "chief men among the brethren" (15:22).

That is the kind of man Silas was—recognized by those who knew him best as a gifted leader of the people of God. He is also called a prophet in verse 32, and it is noted that he preached to the church in Antioch. He liked what was going on in that vital center of faith and service so much that he stayed on even after Judas Barsabas had returned (v. 34).

Silas was no novice in the Early Church. He had earned his place. When Paul and Barnabas disagreed about Mark going on that second missionary journey, Paul knew whom he wanted as his companion in place of Barnabas. It was Silas, his friend. He was a good man, and God's work is always in need of good men.

We don't know anything more about the invitation than what is said in 15:40. Evidently Paul said, "Would you?" and Silas said, "I would." After all, it sounded exciting: to be chosen by the number one man of the church to be his partner; to be out there where the action of faith was on the cutting edge of the church, out there where miracles were occurring and where the glory of redemption was taking place.

So the dream was born. It was not in the plan when he left Jerusalem with a safe and simple mission of certifying a decision of the committee at headquarters. But it was exciting and challenging.

Everybody is looking for promising moments just like that. Sometimes, just like Silas, we don't get what we bargained for!

II. A Man of Bitter Pain

Acts 16 tells us that the teenager Timothy joined them in Lystra (v. 3), and their plans to tour Asia Minor were abruptly changed. A vision in the night pointed them to Greece. They were joined by Dr. Luke (v. 10). Already the plan was different from what Silas had first been told, but still he was undoubtedly sure it would all work out.

Over in Greece they began at Philippi, witnessed the conversion of Lydia, and established their headquarters at her home. But the healing of the demon-possessed girl stirred up opposition from her masters who charged them with disturbing the peace (vv. 19 ff.). The rulers stripped them of their clothing, beat them severely, and threw them in prison—where they were pinned in stocks, unable to move.

I don't know about you, but if I had been there I would probably have been thinking to myself, if not saying aloud, "Now, look at this mess you got us into. Why did I let you talk me into this? It would have been better for me if I had gone back to Jerusalem with Judas." Nobody ever suggested to Silas that part of the journey would be a bloody back and a miserable prison. That was never a part of the plan.

The Christian walk is sometimes like that for all of us—unexpected demands of discipleship, unplanned events of disappointment or discouragement. Charles Colson has chided modern evangelical Christianity with glossing over the demands of discipleship in its pursuit of converts. I remember a new Christian mother struggling to keep her faith vibrant and her five children and errant husband together. She said to me one day, "Pastor, it is hard to be a Christian sometimes. We must tell people that." She was right. God has not promised "skies always blue." Faith that is not adequate for the hard places will not endure.

One of the remarkable passages in the Bible is Acts 16:25 where we read that at "midnight Paul and Silas prayed, and sang praises unto God." One might expect that of Paul; after all, that mission trip was his project. But Silas could have turned the air blue with accusation and self-pity. He did not. Rather he joined his partner in prayer and praise. Praise for what? For God himself; for His promises of presence; for Lydia and other converts like her; for hope for deliverance.

It is interesting that the earthquake and the open doors came after the midnight praise and prayer time, not before it. The marvelous conversion of the Philipppian jailer came after that bitter hour of trust, not before it. It is also interesting that there was an audience to all this—the other prisoners. They saw the actions of Paul and Silas under pressure. They witnessed the jailer's response. Don't you know there was some serious thinking going on behind those prison walls!

III. A Man of Blessed Purpose

We don't hear much more in the Scripture from Silas, or even about him. He continued with Paul and Timothy to Thessalonica, Berea, Athens, and Corinth. Paul names him as his companion in his greetings to the Thessalonians (1 Thess. 1:1), and Peter mentions him as a faithful brother (1 Pet. 5:12). Just because the references are few does not dim the memory of Silas, for we know he did not bail out when life was hard. We honor him because when, as Reuben Welch put it, "life ran out of fantastic, he persevered." We remember him as one whose bright dreams were etched with hard places, and as one who, by enduring those hard places, discovered his own deeper understanding of God, His presence, His power, and His purpose.

I have an idea that when the years were passed and Silas thought back on his Christian life, though he would not have chosen to go through it again, he would not have missed it for anything. For at the end of himself God then revealed himself in a way that Silas could never have anticipated.

It is never easy to sing in midnight prisons. But Silas reminds us that it is possible. As we endure, God enables.

Frances Ridley Havergal was born into a British rectory. Her mother died when Frances was 11. The mother's last words to her daughter were, "Fanny, dear, pray to God to prepare you for all that He is preparing for you." Part of that burden was impaired health, physical suffering, and death in the prime of her life. But her hymns have touched us with power: "I Gave My Life for Thee," "Take My Life, and Let It Be," and many others. The strength of her yielded life shines through the words she wrote:

I take this pain, Lord Jesus, from Thine own hand;
The strength to bear it bravely Thou wilt command.
I take this pain, Lord Jesus; what Thou dost choose
That Thou art watching closely my truest need;

That Thou, my good Physician, art watching still;
That all Thine own good pleasure Thou wilt fulfill.
I take this pain, Lord Jesus; what Thou dost choose
The soul that really loves Thee will not refuse.[1]

Silas would have understood that.

10

Aquila and Priscilla:
Faith Is a Family Affair

Acts 18:1-3, 18-19, 24-26

How important is the home to the church, the family of the flesh to the family of the faith? The truth is that nobody makes it to heaven on his own. We are so wrapped up in each other that none of us is a solo. Rather, we are a part of a chorus, either helping or hurting each other.

One of the functions of the family is not only the imprinting of an ancestry but also the bestowal of a heritage. In the will of God it is the transmitting of a holy heritage of godliness and Christlikeness. It is a heritage that builds a bridge by which we come to Jesus Christ. Church history talks about it: Samuel and Susanna Wesley with that large family of theirs that included the gifted John and Charles; Monica and Augustine; missionaries Nelson and Virginia Bell, and their daughter Ruth who fell in love with and married a young man named Billy Graham. You see, faith at its best is a family affair.

I often wish the Bible told us more about the working of faith in the godly families of old, particularly in the New Testament. The Old Testament with its wide time span and its detailed narratives has glimpses of it—sometimes troubled and sometimes triumphant: Abraham and Sarah; David and Michal; Job and his wife. But in the New Testament with its narrow time span and sharper focus on the saving work of Jesus Christ, there is precious little detail given about family and family members. We are told that Peter was married, but his wife is not named. The house of Cornelius believed on Christ with him, but we are not told who or how many. Timothy had a Christian mother and grandmother in Lois and Eunice, but we don't know anything about his father except that he was an unbelieving Greek. Acts 21 reveals that some early Christians brought their wives and children to a farewell meeting for Paul. We do gain little notes here and there.

But wait! There is a couple in the New Testament who take their place as a kind of model for Christian couples of all time. Aquila and Priscilla speak of faith in the home and of godliness as a family affair. We add them to our list.

I. TOGETHER IN SUFFERING

We know nothing of their backgrounds except that Aquila was a Jew born in Pontus, a region of what is now Turkey near the eastern end of the Black Sea. We also know that Rome had been home for both him and his wife. Beyond that there is historical silence. What matters for them and for us is not so much what was before Jesus but what happens with Jesus. It is Jesus who, in the light of eternity, makes somebodies out of nobodies.

We do not know what took Aquila to Rome. We can only speculate about the events in the lives of this couple: about the romance that brought the two together, about the record of success or failure that was theirs in that fabled city 19 centuries ago, about the dream they were building there, about business, relationships, and all the other things that enter into our lives. Whatever they were, life came crashing down around them the day the decree went out from Emperor Claudius commanding every Jew to leave Rome.

It is there in the history books. Suetonius says in his work on the life of Claudius that the Emperor "expelled the Jews from Rome because they were in a state of continual tumult at the instigation of one Chrestus"—undoubtedly meaning Christ.[1] The resentment of the Jewish community to the Christian witness took its toll.

As best we know, Aquila and Priscilla never planned to be in Corinth. It was the backwash of a broken dream, the consequence of matters beyond their control. Maybe I am reading more into the record than is there, but just maybe that is exactly the way it was. What if each of us was faced with an edict of government that demanded relocation in some distant place within 30 days? It is hard to imagine—forced sale at tremendous if not total loss; removal from friends; abandonment of house and home. When World War II broke out, America experienced something of that when the presidential decree ordered Japanese Americans into remote relocation camps. In my first congregation there was a Japanese American family who had been caught in that troubled time. Their firstborn son was delivered in the stable of a racetrack near San Francisco while they waited for orders that would take them to a place they had never been and to which they did not want to go.

I have to believe that it was hard on Aquila and Priscilla, but they did not let it destroy them or their relationship. Evidently, they did allow it to deepen them and their commitment to each other. Life is full of hard things that we think ought not to be, especially for the child of God. And even if our heads get it worked out, our hearts struggle.

But the hard place that can destroy can also strengthen, if God is at work and life is surrendered to Him. God was at work in the lives of Aquila and Priscilla. They had to go somewhere. They chose Corinth, commercial center of Greece, bustling seaport of business and trade. It turned out to be the move that later on they would thank God for as the best thing that ever happened to them. How often the hard place is just like that. Down the road we will know that God used it, and we would not have missed it for all the world.

II. TOGETHER IN SHARING

First, this couple shared their home with a preacher named Paul (18:3). It was second missionary journey time for Paul. He left Athens feeling somewhat defeated; he went to Corinth resolved to preach Jesus Christ and Him crucified (1 Cor. 2:2). He went alone; Silas and Timothy would join him later. To supply his needs he worked at his trade of tentmaking. That brought him into contact with Aquila and Priscilla, who were also of that occupation, and they shared their home with him.

Were Aquila and Priscilla Christians when they went to Corinth? Luke does not say. The commentaries are not persuaded. Perhaps they were. I like to think they were not. I like to think they were a good couple, mellowed by life's hard places, hungering for God, led by the providences of God into the friendship of a man who could tell them and show them how to find God in Jesus Christ.

Were they Christians when they went to Corinth? You decide. But the really important thing is that when they left Corinth, they were Christians—rooted and grounded, saved and sanctified, committed to Christ for the long journey. Why? Because they had been touched by someone who knew Jesus.

Second, in Ephesus they shared their faith with Apollos (Acts 18:24-26). He was a gifted speaker from Africa, long on eloquence but short on spiritual understanding. "They invited him to their home and explained . . . the way of God more adequately" (v. 26, NIV). They discipled him—that's what they did. They invested their lives in him and helped him so that he might help others.

Aquila and Priscilla shared their home, their heart, and their faith. They literally gave themselves away. The glory of it, the power of it, was that they did it *together.* It was not one or the other; it was both. It was "we." Never once in the record of Aquila and Priscilla is the reference singular. In every mention they are both named. Sometimes the husband first and then the wife; sometimes the wife first and then the husband. It was they—their home, their faith.

What does it take to share? It takes time, sacrifice, prayer, and love. The price is high. But it is best done as they did it— together. And in God's own time, the blessings come back to us.

III. Together in Serving

Lest we get the feeling that the pouring out of their lives in Acts 18 was an impulse that soon faded, or an excitement that quickly died because the price was too high or the demand too great, look with me at the other references to this Christian couple of old.

As to its date, 1 Cor. 16:19 was written about five years later. Paul was writing back to the church in Corinth—the work of Christ that began when Paul came, made tents, and preached Christ for a year and a half, and stayed with a husband and wife named Aquila and Priscilla. What a great beginning. And as he closes his letter, written from Ephesus, he says, "The churches of Asia salute you. Aquila and Priscilla salute you much in the Lord, with *the church that is in their house*" (italics added).

You see they had caught the thrill of ministry. They made tents for a living, but they lived to serve Christ. Their home was His home, whether in Corinth where it began or in Ephesus where they moved. Their house became a center of Christian fellowship, and they did it together.

Next is Rom. 16:3. The time was about a year after 1 Cor. 16:19; approximately six years after Acts 18. The decree of Claudius had been lifted. And now we find Aquila and Priscilla back in Rome. This time, they are there on a mission. The Christ they had met elsewhere they had taken back with them. The passage is thrilling: "Greet Priscilla and Aquila my helpers in Christ Jesus: who have for my life laid down their own necks: unto whom not only I give thanks, but also all the churches of the Gentiles. Likewise greet *the church that is in their house* . . ." (Rom. 16:3-5, italics added). No wonder Paul loved them. They had put their lives on the line for him. They had done it for others, too, and as usual their house was His.

Finally there is the passage in 2 Tim. 4:19. About 15 years have now passed. Paul is writing his last letter. Execution is at hand. He writes final instructions to Timothy, in charge of the church at Ephesus. As he closes he sends one final, single greeting. "Salute Prisca [Priscilla] and Aquila, and the household of Onesiphorus."

By now they have gone back to Ephesus, partly perhaps due to the persecution of Nero; partly perhaps to help Timothy with the ministry there where years earlier they too had opened their house and invested their lives.

The power of it was that it was not just "him" and not just "her," but it was "them." They are examples of a long list of those who tell us that faith at its best is indeed a "family affair."

11

Apollos:
Going Beyond Our Gifts

Acts 18:24-28; 1 Cor. 1:12; 3:5-6; 16:12

Not long ago, my son and I spent a few hours in the buildings of our state capital in Sacramento, Calif. A young man from our church, Rob Stutzman, who was a summer intern in the governor's office, pointed out things of interest that pertained to our state's chief executive. We sat for a while in the gallery of both the state Senate and state Assembly, tried to identify names and faces as bills were debated and votes were taken. I tried to grasp it all. These men are the movers and shakers of our society—the largest state in our nation, the seventh largest economic enterprise in the world.

I thought to myself that there is a craft, a skill to the business of politics, to government and administration. But what of the work of God? Is it done on exactly the same basis as the business of politics, driven by the same forces that power the machinery of government? My answer had to be, no. For while the work of God needs the best of human wisdom and the finest of human talent, that, in and of itself, is not enough. Long ago God said through Zechariah, "Not by might, nor by power, but by my spirit, saith the Lord of hosts" (4:6). It is only when what we are at our best is touched, cleansed, controlled, and guided by the Holy Spirit that we become usable tools in the building of God's eternal kingdom. It is only as we discover and know the life of God for ourselves that we can become channels of the life of God for others who need Him so desperately.

That is the message of Apollos. Matthias speaks of faithfulness; Barnabas of encouragement; and each of the previous second-string heroes exemplifies a particular quality of character. In this study Apollos trumpets the truth that those who would really be His must go beyond their natural gifts into the life of the Spirit himself.

I. APOLLOS: SOMETHING MISSING

Apollos appears suddenly on the stage of Bible history. Paul had left Ephesus to return to Jerusalem (which would complete his second missionary journey) when Apollos arrived in that city on the western coast of what is now the nation of Turkey.

The brief background of verse 24 is all we really know of him. He came from Alexandria, the second greatest city in the Roman Empire. It had been founded by Alexander the Great on the north coast of Egypt, just west of the Nile. It was a center of learning and education, with quite possibly the largest settlement of Jews outside of the land of Palestine. There in Alexandria the Hebrew Scriptures had been translated into Greek some 200 years earlier, opening the door of the Bible to the Gentile world.

With that kind of heritage we can better understand and accept the grand tribute paid to Apollos in verse 24 that he was a man of great natural gifts, "an eloquent man, and mighty in the scriptures." *The Living Bible* translates that as, "a wonderful Bible teacher and preacher."

In short, Apollos was one of life's gifted ones, one of the

"winners." Both heredity and environment had brought out the best graces in him. He was the kind of fellow who would have made it well in any field. No wonder that later when Aquila and Priscilla heard him, they were drawn to him. No wonder that later as he preached in Corinth there would be many who ranked him No. 1, even to the point of arguing over it. He was gifted as few men ever are.

Second, note that in addition to his natural gifts Apollos also possessed a sincere spiritual desire. He had a mind for the Scriptures. That is what is said of him. He knew them for what they said of a Messiah, of a call to repentance, and of a return to God. He knew them for what they said of things to come. What a great combination: natural ability and moral concern. Apollos had leadership gifts and an inclination toward religion that made him bold to speak out, even in a new community like Ephesus. He declared God's unchanging call to righteousness and God's great promise of a Redeemer.

Even with all of his assets, Apollos was missing something. It was the dynamic of a personal relationship with God in Jesus Christ, an experience of redemption that was both born of the Spirit and filled with the Spirit. The language of verse 25 is confusing, as it says that he "taught diligently the things of the Lord, knowing only the baptism of John." This is the same condition as the disciples described in 19:3. The baptism of John meant two things: a repentant spirit that wanted God and an expectant heart toward the Messiah of God. So that is where I understand Apollos to have been, religiously sincere and believing somehow that Jesus was the Sent One of God, that far and no farther. He did not know the dynamic of a personal walk with Jesus, nor the reality of the Holy Spirit who makes Jesus real and the heart clean. Apollos, in my mind, was not unlike John Wesley before his own heart-warming experience.

Apollos was an example of the best of the human family

on their own—great intentions, high purpose, strong discipline, religious earnestness, but ultimate spiritual emptiness. He was not the last man to have everything but God. He was not the last man to try hard, only to discover that simply trying hard can never be enough.

II. APOLLOS: SOMETHING FOUND

Who can understand the providences of God? They are beyond our comprehension but not beyond our praise. In Ephesus, the motivated Apollos continued as a voice for religion in the place of worship, an encyclopedia of reference here and insight there. In the congregation that noble couple Aquila and Priscilla heard him. They heard what he said and what he did not say, and they were impressed. They sensed that God was wanting them to take Apollos as their discipling project, and they did. They took him to themselves and "expounded unto him the way of God more perfectly" (v. 26).

What does that mean? I believe it means they shared with Apollos the full record of the life, death, and resurrection of Jesus Christ since the time of John, in case he had not heard it all. I believe they instructed him in the coming and the ministry of the Holy Spirit in clear terms both of being born of the Spirit and of being filled with the Spirit. I think they told him what Jesus had done in their own lives and what He could do in his.

Aquila and Priscilla "discerned" and "discipled." The need of the world is to find the Lord, and the assignment of believers is to discern those to whom the Lord is speaking and then to evangelize and disciple them. This is true both at the beginning point of conversion and the deeper crisis of cleansing. Thank God for those whose spiritual antennae are so tuned that they can sense the cry, and whose hearts are so full that they have the bread of life to share. Apollos needed help even though he did not know it. But one Christian couple perceived it and moved in with arms of love, not in judgment that turns people off but in affirmation that lifts people up. In the long view of history, they gave Apollos to the Church.

III. APOLLOS: SOMETHING PROCLAIMED

Apollos went to Ephesus an unbeatable debater, but he left Ephesus an established Spirit-filled witness. When he came people were impressed with his knowledge; when he left they were impressed with his Savior. When he came people backed away from his boldness, but when he left they were attracted to his Christlikeness. Why? Because he came to understand that his gifts, however many, were not enough. He needed one more gift—the gift of spiritual life in the person of Jesus by the power of the Holy Spirit.

His new life in Christ was affirmed by the Christians in Ephesus who "encouraged him." They believed in Apollos. They wrote letters on his behalf (Acts 18:17). They said, in essence, "This Apollos is a good man; he is for real; God has changed him; let him share his testimony with you; he will do you good."

And Apollos found a new ministry in Christ. The words of 1 Cor. 1:12 and 3:5-6 tell how he went to that city and ministered mightily. Such was his impact that people argued over just who was the greatest of the Christian preachers—Peter or Paul or Apollos. (Paul would write that greatness was not the issue—for every man has a place to fill that Jesus might be lifted up.)

When the years had passed, the last mention of Apollos came from Paul in his letter to Titus, living on the island of Crete, to help Apollos on his journey as a man on a mission for the Lord (Titus 3:13).

What made the difference in his life? Was it not that he

came to a place where he realized something was missing from his life, namely the reality of full salvation, and then came to his own experience in Christ, both of Spirit-newness and Spirit-fullness? And out of these his natural gifts were quickened for holy service, and he became fruitful in the kingdom of God.

It still can happen; it still must happen—people hungering for more of God and discovering more of God. And it does happen. Not long ago a retired mortician and his wife, Louis and Barbara Edmunds, moved to our community and began to attend our church. They asked me to come to their home, where they spoke of years of religious activity and sincerity, but of deep inward emptiness. In response to the Bible's offer of a fullness of the Spirit they knelt in their home to make full surrender of their lives to Christ by the Holy Spirit. They wrote a note that said, "Our whole outlook on life has changed to a degree you would not imagine since we rededicated our lives to Christ, and are studying His Word, spending time in prayer, and making a strong effort to walk closer to the Lord."

At the end of ourselves is the beginning of himself. He waits to be wanted. Let Him not wait in vain.

12

Luke:
A Labor of Love

Acts 16:6–15; Col. 4:14; Philem. 24; 2 Tim. 4:11

In our world there is the ever-present temptation to associate worth with public recognition and to equate greatness with fame. The consequence can be invalidating, making heroes of sometimes hollow men. The flip side is to equate ordinariness with worthlessness.

But in the eyes of God, the measure of our lives is not the headlines we grab but the obedience we display, a labor for Christ and His kingdom motivated more than anything else by our simple, honest, daily commitment to Him.

I am impressed with that ancient Christian, Dr. Luke. He surely has a place in this series of second-string heroes but first-class saints. Luke, the great but modest physician, speaks about what happens when "they" becomes "we." Luke reveals the Christian labor of love.

I. A MISSION TO SHARE

Luke is never even named in the Book of Acts, though he wrote it. We trace him, not by his naming of himself but by the pronouns . . . when the language shifts from "they" and "them" and "he" and "him" to "we" and "us." Indeed, Luke is only named three times in the Scripture, and that always by

Paul: Philem. 24; 2 Tim. 4:11; Col. 4:14. In that last reference Paul calls him "beloved physician."

Luke, a Greek and the only Gentile to share in the writing of the New Testament, was a doctor by profession, but he became a Christian by choice. He practiced medicine for a living, but there came the day when he decided to live to serve Christ.

We really do not know the background of Luke's life. Beyond the reference to his physician status, we have to sift it from subtle notes of Scripture. We do not know for sure just how or when he came to Christ. Acts 16 tells us that Paul, Silas, and Timothy on that second missionary journey had plans to evangelize western Asia Minor, but their plans seemed to collapse. Verse 6 says they "were forbidden of the Holy Ghost to preach the word in Asia." God had evidently said no to their plans in order to inaugurate His better plan. Twice it says the door was closed (vv. 6-7). But when God closes some doors He opens others.

Some think that Paul was ill; that he sought out a doctor; that that doctor, a man of intellect, grace, and culture who knew the poverty of wealth and the emptiness of status, heard the Christian witness of the apostle and believed on Jesus. They suggest that he talked with Paul about taking the Christian message over into Greece. Just maybe, they suggest, the vision Paul had in the night of a man from Macedonia saying, "Come over and help us," was born of his relationship with a Greek doctor who became a Christian and said, "My country and my people need to know this."

That is conjecture, but this is fact. Somewhere, Luke put his life into the hands of Christ, and when he did there was no turning back.

In Acts 16:10, the "they" becomes "we." The Christian mission did not just belong to Paul, Silas, and Timothy. It was Luke's also, and he would give it the best he had.

So follow the "we." "We" went to Philippi (v. 12); "we"

went to the place of prayer at the riverside; "we" shared Jesus; "we" talked with a woman named Lydia who opened her heart to the Lord and invited "us" to stay at her home.

When Paul and Silas were jailed, then released and had left Philippi, Luke evidently stayed behind. The "we" passages cease until Paul came again (20:5) and then continue to the end of the Book of Acts. Luke was there when the prisoner Paul sailed for Rome. He was there when the ship wrecked on the Mediterranean island of Malta. He was there when Paul met the murderous sword of Rome. Why? Because when he determined to go with Jesus, he determined to go all the way.

When Jesus really takes ownership of us, when we really give ourselves to Him, then His mission becomes our mission. The "they" becomes "we." The devil will try to keep that from happening. He will shout the merits of keeping a safe distance from the field of spiritual battle and labor. But if we are truly His, we have no choice.

Some of God's best voices warn us against the temptation to try to make salvation a matter of accepting the gift but rejecting His mission. A. W. Tozer did it passionately. Charles Colson has stung the modern church with the indictment. Dr. Dennis Kinlaw has reminded us that Jesus' most common call to discipleship was not "accept Me" but "follow Me."

So the question always facing the professing Christian is not only about his commitment to the person of Christ but equally about his commitment to the work of Christ. Has the "they" become "we"?

II. A Message to Search

Luke did more than just join in to tag along, as good as that was. Luke dug in deeply, he studied hard, he equipped himself for service, and in the process equipped the church for ministry also.

He was not an eyewitness of the events of the life, death, and resurrection of Jesus Christ. But he wanted to know—for sure. He thirsted for knowledge. God used his special intelligence, his keen mind and cultured training, and his hunger for truth—just as God will with us if we let Him. In Luke's case, the legacy to us is the Gospel of Luke and the Book of Acts. The witness of the Church throughout history has been unanimous in his authorship.

In Luke 1:1-4 Luke writes that others had written of the ministry of Christ who were eyewitnesses. But he confesses that he had traced the records from the beginning and was writing to Theophilus, that he also might be certain. Luke wanted others to be as sure of Jesus as he himself was.

And then in Acts 1:1-4, Luke takes up his pen to write to Theophilus again, this time to complete the record of the things that Jesus began to do and teach, taking us from His ascension and Pentecost to Paul's imprisonment in Rome.

Some think that while Paul was in jail at Caesarea for those two years, Luke used the time to research the records with eyewitnesses like the disciples and wrote the Gospel of Luke not long thereafter. Some think that while Paul was under house arrest in Rome, Luke recorded the history of Pentecost and the expansion of the Early Church. Perhaps both were to be documents used in the defense of Paul before Rome.

But the point is this: Luke claimed as his own all that God had done. He examined the data; he tasted for himself. He was neither Jew nor eyewitness, but he would be sure. He used words like "certainty" (Luke 1:4) and "proofs" (Acts 1:3). He searched it, and it was his. No wonder God used him. He equipped himself, and that is why we are still indebted to him. We never read that Luke preached, as Paul did. But we read from him what Paul preached—and what Jesus taught. God comes to us through him who searched the message and made it his own.

Hard? Yes. It was a labor, but it was a labor of love. An invitation of Jesus is still wide open for whosoever will to join in.

III. A MINISTRY TO SUSTAIN

It is one thing to begin with zeal, but it is another thing to finish in faithfulness. Luke, who began so gloriously by sharing the mission and recording the history, never did turn back or give up. The three references by Paul are all a decade or more later, written from Rome where Paul endured the house arrest referred to in Acts 28.

Paul wrote to Philemon about his runaway slave Onesimus who had become a Christian under Paul's ministry in Rome. He closed by sending the greetings of his fellow laborers. The last named is Luke (Philem. 24).

He wrote to the church in Colosse, where Philemon lived, and included the greetings of his companion, "Luke, the beloved physician" (Col. 4:14).

In Paul's last letter, just before his death in Rome, he wrote to Timothy, the young pastor of the church at Ephesus. He gave instructions and encouragement. He also asked Timothy to come to him in Rome and to do it "before winter" (2 Tim. 4:21). His statement was, "Only Luke is with me" (v. 11).

The years have passed—some 15 of them probably. Luke is older. But he is as committed, yea, more so, as the day he first made the cause of Jesus his own.

That is the way it is with the people of God. Velma Mischke, retired missionary, lives in a convalescent hospital in my community, her body twisted by the effects of a stroke. She talks about giving Jesus the best years of her life when she and her husband served the Lord, the church, and mankind as missionaries in Africa. Those days are far behind her now. But still there is in her heart the longing to be useful to the Lord. She told me one day about one of the young aides in the hospital asking her, "How does one know that she is called to Christian service?" Velma told her, "I guess that is why I am here, to help others." She added, "I tell the Lord, when I can't help others anymore, take me home."

13

Paul:
The Man Least Likely

Acts 9:1–31

It took place in July of 1986. The annual Major League All-Star game brought together the best players from both leagues. Among them was Don Mattingly, outstanding first baseman for the New York Yankees, consistent performer, always near the top in every category from home runs, to runs batted in, to batting average. What caught the attention of the news media in a special way, however, was not just the presence of Don Mattingly but one of the bats that he brought with him.

On the Yankee roster in 1986 was a utility infielder—Mike Fischlin—whose batting average was less than .200, with no home runs, only 3 runs batted in, and only occasional playing time. He had said to Mattingly, "Since I will probably never play in an all-star game, would you mind using my bat just so I could feel a part of it?" The sportscaster who reported that incident, chuckled: "Probably? With statistics like that, not just probably, but never!"

But what if a player like that, one least likely to succeed, went on to achieve star status the next year?

The conclusion of this series focuses on the apostle Paul. Had we been living in his time, we would have rated him the man least likely to become a member of God's great team, least likely to take a stand for Jesus, least likely to become a spokesman of the gospel. In Paul we see the transforming power of the gospel of Christ. How else can we account for the fact that the man least likely became the man best known and the most widely used. That fact is the continuing reminder that nobody is outside the invitation of Jesus to come to Him and find in Him transformation through redeeming grace.

I. GOD WOULD NOT LET HIM GO

Unlike most of the other second-string heroes of Acts, we know a great deal about Paul. Born in Tarsus, university trained under Gamaliel, the most respected rabbi of the day, Paul was a brilliant and gifted young man of two worlds— Greek in culture, training, and thinking, but Jewish in religion, ethics, and legalism. A Hebrew through and through from the small tribe of Benjamin, he took the disciplined road of the Pharisees—committed to the whole code of Jewish legalism and all that it demanded. Little wonder, then, that he saw in the claim of Jesus and in the message of the gospel heresy, blasphemy, and the destruction of all he held dear. He was, by choice and by office, the official overseer of the lynching of Stephen that launched him on a holy war against the followers of Jesus. He started it at Jerusalem, and when that persecution scattered believers, Paul pursued them everywhere and anywhere. That is why he was going to Damascus (Acts 9:1-2), a journey of 150 miles to the north of Jerusalem—a journey of a week each way. He had warrants for the arrest and extradition of any Christian he might find there.

That is the background of the greatest theologian, missionary, and preacher the church has ever known. He was indeed in that hour the man of whom we would have said, "On God's team?—never; anyone, but not Paul!"

Behold the grace of God. Something happened that Paul had not taken into account. Jesus met him and mastered him, and that made all the difference.

Luke does not tell us all that was going on in Paul's mind as he journeyed northward. But we may well understand that in those months of his continuing vendetta against the faith, there was a growing mass of conviction in Paul's heart. He had seen Stephen die unjustly with forgiveness on his lips. I think that made an impact on him he never forgot. He had observed that persecution did not destroy these Christians. He had heard his revered teacher Gamaliel hint before the Jewish senate that just maybe it might all be of God, and if that were so, then nobody could stop it (Acts 5:39). With that kind of input, there was a nagging question he could not share with anyone. Those early Christians had found in Jesus a peace, purpose, power, and love that Paul must have ached for in his restless but unfulfilling pursuit of law.

Conviction is what we call it. God is too good to let anyone do wrong and feel right about it. He keeps calling in the jungle of life, "You were made for something better . . . come home . . . I made you for myself."

So it was, on the outskirts of Damascus, one of the oldest cities of the world, Paul met Christ in a blinding flash of light that made him stop, with a directness that made him listen. The Christ he had so vehemently denied met him face-to-face. God would not let him go.

Paul would never be the same again. Later he would call himself "one born out of due time" (1 Cor. 15:8). He would speak often of that noon on that highway. Why not? From that moment on he was a new man under new orders—to "get up and go . . . you will be told what you must do" (Acts 9:6, NIV).

Not all conversions are as dramatic as Paul's. Some are soft and gradual like the sunrise. Timothy's was like that—with the influence of a Christian mother and grandmother and the gentle choice of Jesus in young years. Some conversions are quiet, like Lydia's—a good moral person responding sincerely to the new light of the gospel. But some conversions are spectacular, such as Paul's—a 180 degree turn from going all out away from Christ to going all out for Christ.

All conversions, whether quiet, gentle, or spectacular, are basically the same, for in conversion Jesus moves from the outside of life to the inside of life, making God real and making men whole.

In truth, it is those who are most likely to be saved who will be saved. That is why it is so important to build Christian families and bring children up in Sunday School and church. In truth, those least likely to be saved are least likely to be saved. But also, in truth, there is a grace in Jesus that can reach the most unlikely. Therefore we dare not count anyone out. Every man, no matter who he is, is a candidate for God's amazing grace.

II. GOD WOULD NOT LET HIM DOWN

The story of Paul in Damascus is told in verses 10-19. He was blind and confused and so much in need of the ministry of comfort and counsel that came to him from Ananias. If it is true that the Church owes Paul to the prayer of Stephen, it is also true that the Church owes Paul to the brotherliness of Ananias. One kind of crisis ended for Paul on the Damascus road, but another kind of crisis began. Newborn Christians need the same kind of care that newborn babies do. Without it they do what newborn babies do—they die. That is why God put His hand on Ananias. Paul needed help, and God would not let him down.

Note four things about Ananias:

First, he was available. Verse 10 says that when God

called him, Ananias heard and responded, "I am here, Lord." It is not just our ability but our availability that God seeks.

Second, Ananias was assignable. God's directions were very specific—to the street, to the house, to the person in prayer. When God works, he does so on both ends. He dealt with Paul, but he also dealt with the one to help Paul. The whole conversion of Paul might have been lost had it not been for the godly consecration and obedience of Ananias. He was willing to embrace with loving arms someone in need of him.

Third, Ananias was adjustable. The fears of Ananias were real (v. 13). He knew about Paul and why he had come. Indeed perhaps the name of Ananias was on the list in Paul's pocket. But Ananias was willing to believe God that Paul was a chosen man in whom God was at work.

Fourth, Ananias was accountable. In some of the most moving words of Scripture the humble Christian of Damascus said, "Brother Saul, the Lord, even Jesus . . . hath sent me" (v. 17). Ananias went with the power of God to touch blinded eyes that they might see. He went with the love of God to embrace as a brother one who had been an enemy. And the one who had come as a persecutor became a preacher in Damascus, to the amazement of everyone (vv. 20-21).

None of us can save anyone, but each of us can help nurture the faith and walk of someone whom Jesus has saved. Without Ananias, or someone like him, the man least likely to be saved would have become the man most likely to have given up.

III. GOD WOULD NOT LET HIM OFF

God had a mission for Paul; he was indeed a chosen instrument in the plan of God. Though Luke does not tell the whole story, the sequence of events went something like this:

1. In Damascus Paul began immediately to tell of his new faith and commitment (v. 20). In a short time, however, he real-

ized he had to think his new commitment through, so he went into isolation in Arabia (Gal. 1:17).

2. After waiting on God in that solitary setting and thinking through the meaning of the gospel and its scope of truth, he came again into Damascus and preached more boldly. Time passed. Opposition arose. He was hurried out of the city to escape a murder plot. He went to Jerusalem. Galatians 1 says it was some three years after he had set out for Damascus.

3. In Jerusalem, things were tense. The Jews considered him a traitor, and the Christians feared him as a spy. Barnabas, in his characteristic way, was the one to build the bridge of trust and acceptance (v. 27). When another plot against him was discovered, Paul was secreted out of town and back to his home in Tarsus.

4. In Tarsus the months turned into years. We assume that Paul made tents for a living and honed the fine points of Christian faith and doctrine, perhaps quietly sharing his faith with others. It was about 6 years later, nearly a full 10 years after he had set out for Damascus, that Barnabas, the encourager, with a burden on his heart for the flourishing work of Jesus at Antioch, sought out Paul in Tarsus, saying, "God has a world to reach . . . you are His man . . . that is why He saved you . . . there is a place in Antioch that needs you." And you know the rest of the story.

We are here because the man least likely to find Christ did find Christ. He formed the solid foundations of Christian doctrine; he planted the church where it had never been; 13 of the 27 parts of the New Testament bear his signature. All from a man of whom most of us would have said, "Never!"

All of that suggests two things:

If you think you are the person least likely, don't be too sure. God specializes in miracles of transformation.

If you know someone whom you think is the person least likely, don't give up. If God did it before, surely God can do it again.

Suggested Discussion Questions

In case the text is used for a Sunday School class or another kind of study group, the following questions are offered as aids to class discussion.

Chapter 1

1. Think of the people whom God has used to influence your life for Christ. What were the qualities of those lives that impressed you? How did it occur?
2. Were those people well-known or little-known? What does that say to you?
3. Were they faithful Christians? What does that say to you?
4. What are the keys to faithfulness in Christ?

Chapter 2

1. What kind of person do you think Barnabas was? Why? What attributes do you see in him?
2. Do you think the Early Church gave him leadership because of his gift of money to the Church? Why? Why not?
3. Can all people exercise the ministry of encouragement, or is it a special gift that only a few have?
4. Can you share out of your life about someone who has helped you with the touch of encouragement that has made the difference? Can you do the same for another?
5. Have you tried to encourage anyone this week?

Chapter 3

1. What about Stephen speaks to you the most?
2. Of the things recorded about his life, which do you think is the hardest to do and why: (1) wait tables; (2) witness for Christ; (3) forgive those who persecute you?
3. Which of these is most Christlike? Why?
4. Can you see something of Stephen in our congregation?

Chapter 4

1. What do you see as Philip's greatest virtue?
2. What, do you think, was his most difficult assignment of evangelism—the Samaritans (public); the Ethiopian (personal); or his family (private)? Why?
3. Of the six reasons listed for not witnessing, which one troubles you the most and why? Which one, do you think, reflects the greatest numbers of people?

Chapter 5

1. Why, do you think, did God select Cornelius to be the first of the Gentile converts to enter the New Covenant in Christ?
2. What about him impresses you the most and why?
3. How do we nurture the hunger for holiness in ourselves? In others?

Chapter 6

1. Why, do you think, did Mark leave the missionary journey of Paul and Barnabas? Was he right or wrong in doing so?
2. Why, do you think, did Paul oppose the involvement of Mark in the next mission journey so vigorously? Was it that big an issue, really?

3. How do you explain Mark's ultimate effectiveness in the light of his seeming failure?
4. What does Mark say to you, personally?

Chapter 7

1. Describe in your own words the homelife Timothy had. Spiritually speaking, who was the most influential person in his life—mother, grandmother, father?
2. Think about your own home and childhood. Who was most influential in shaping your life? If you have children, can you see the reflection of your life in them?
3. What was it that Paul saw in Timothy that moved him to invite Timothy to join his ministry team?
4. How do you understand Timothy's personality and gifts? Were those weaknesses a hindrance to ministry or were they used of God as a complement to Paul's ministry? Does God use different gifts in His service? How? Why?
5. Are you more like Paul or like Timothy?

Chapter 8

1. Describe the kind of person you think Lydia was.
2. What does it take for any person to be successful in business? Especially for a lady to be successful in business?
3. Where do you think Lydia was in her spiritual life before she heard the gospel?
4. How, do you think, did her life change after she gave her heart to the Lord? What was different? What was not different?
5. What Christian women do you know who remind you of Lydia? Why?

Chapter 9

1. What impresses you the most about Silas and why?
2. Do we tell new Christians enough about the hard things of serving the Lord? Do we tend to "oversell" the gospel in our quest to bring people to Christ?
3. Has your Christian journey held things you did not expect? How have you handled it?
4. How would you have handled the midnight prision situation? (Be honest.)
5. Are there things in your Christian walk that you would never have chosen to go through, but now you would not exchange them for anything? What? Why?

Chapter 10

1. What kind of Christian heritage did you have—or not have? How did it shape you?
2. Can you think of difficult places that you would never have chosen but that God used significantly "for good"? How?
3. What are some obstacles for Christian couples in their mutual service to Christ and the church? How can they handle them?
4. What are some ways in which husbands and wives can serve the Lord and the church together?
5. Do you know couples who remind you of Aquila and Priscilla? Who? Why?

Chapter 11

1. Describe the kind of person you think Apollos was when he came to Ephesus. Do you know people now who are like he was?
2. How, do you think, did Aquila and Priscilla approach Apol-

los in their desire to lead him deeper in the things of God? What did they do? What did they not do?

3. How can we best communicate to the "nominal" Christian that God has more for him?

4. How can we better lead newer Christians into the life of Christian holiness?

Chapter 12

1. Luke researched the Gospel to make it his own. How do we sharpen our faith? How have you strengthened the foundations of your Christian faith?

2. What kind of temperament, do you think, did Luke have? Was he much like Paul or different? What kinds of temperament do we need in the church?

3. Someone has said that there are three commitments for every Christian—to the person of Christ, to the Body of Christ, to the work of Christ. What is the proper order of priority? Where, if any, does the commitment most break down?

4. Do you know people who remind you of Luke? Who? Why?

Chapter 13

1. In your thinking, what played the biggest part in preparing Paul's heart for Christ on the Damascus road: (1) Stephen; (2) the endurance of persecuted Christians; (3) the words of Gamaliel; or (4) something else? Why?

2. What impresses you about the roles played by Ananias and by Barnabas in Paul's spiritual development?

3. Why did it take so long, apparently, for Paul to be used in Christian ministry after his conversion? Was that good or bad?

4. How would you describe the impact of Paul's ministry for Christ? Why was God able to use him so significantly?

5. Is God more impressed with His "superstars" than with his ordinary people? Why or why not? What matters most?

Notes

CHAPTER ONE

1. Charles Wesley, "Times Without Number Have I Pray'd," in *Masterpieces of Religious Verse*, ed. James Dalton Morrison (New York: Harper and Brothers, 1948), 93.

CHAPTER TWO

1. Randal E. Denny, *Do It Again, Lord* (Kansas City: Beacon Hill Press of Kansas City, 1978), 133.

CHAPTER FIVE

1. "Breaking Away," *Sacramento Bee*, June 22, 1986, Magazine section.

2. A. W. Tozer, *The Pursuit of God* (Harrisburg, Pa.: Christian Publications, 1948), 49.

3. D. Shelby Corlett, *God in the Present Tense* (Kansas City: Beacon Hill Press of Kansas City, 1974), 11-12.

CHAPTER SIX

1. Rudyard Kipling, *Rewards and Fairies* (New York: Doubleday and Company, n.d.). Used by permission.

2. A. W. Tozer, *Born After Midnight* (Harrisburg, Pa.: Christian Publications, 1959), 44.

CHAPTER SEVEN

1. "Who's Making Big Bucks?" *Reader's Digest*, January 1988, 118.

CHAPTER NINE

1. W. T. Purkiser, *When You Get to the End of Yourself* (Kansas City: Beacon Hill Press of Kansas City, 1970), 69.

CHAPTER TEN

1. Ralph Earle, *Beacon Bible Commentary* (Kansas City: Beacon Hill Press of Kansas City, 1965), 7:464.